Addicted to Love

Also by Jan Geurtz

De opluchting
De verslaving voorbij
Het einde van de opvoeding
Verslaafd aan denken
Bevrijd door liefde
Vrij van gedachten

Jan Geurtz

Addicted to Love

The path to self-acceptance and happiness in relationships

Translated by Janet Taylor

Ambo|Anthos
Amsterdam

ISBN 978 90 263 3740 6
© 2009 Ambo|Anthos uitgevers, Amsterdam
Original title *Verslaafd aan liefde. De weg naar zelfacceptatie en geluk in relaties*
Cover design Studio Jan de Boer
Fotograph of the author © Kimm Govers

Contents

PART 1
Nothing is as it appears

1 Introduction: the mother of all misunderstandings 11
2 The first layer of our identity: the negative belief 18
3 The second layer of our identity: the basic rules 26
4 The third layer of our identity: patterns in thinking, feeling and behaviour 33
5 The fourth and final layer of our identity: the image 38
6 Disruptions in the development of our identity 44
7 Stagnations in the growth of consciousness 51
8 The creation of suffering 61
9 The free market of love and approval 69
10 The love relationship 75
11 The relationship crisis 84
12 The vicious circle of samsara 95

PART 2
Everything is as it is

13 The spiritual path 101
14 Letting go of 'relationship thinking' 111
15 Looking at your own mind: who is looking? 117

16 Painful emotions: the door to your natural state 127
17 Integration instead of dissociation 136
18 The natural state of being: belief or reality? 144
19 The spiritual love relationship 151
20 Spiritual sex 165
21 Love derailments 177
22 For the sake of the children 185
23 The perfect illusion 191

APPENDIX 1
Sources, recommendations and thanks 199

APPENDIX 2
Western resistance to Eastern spirituality 204

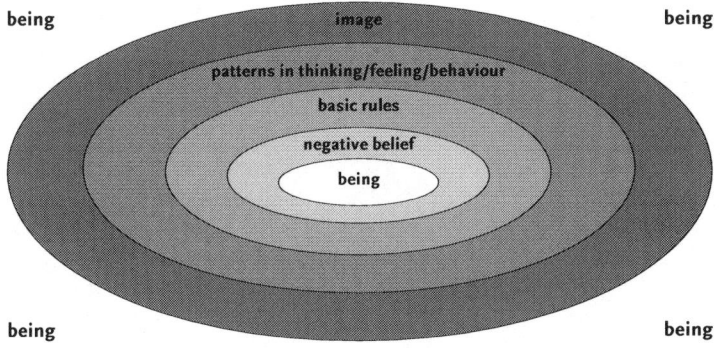

Figure 1: The layers of our identity that cover the natural state of being.

PART 1

Nothing is as it appears

Know all things to be like this:
A mirage, a cloud castle,
A dream, an apparition,
Without essence, but with qualities that can be seen.

Know all things to be like this:
As the moon in a bright sky
In some clear lake reflected,
Though to that lake the moon has never moved.

Know all things to be like this:
As an echo that derives
From music, sounds and weeping,
Yet in that echo is no melody.

Know all things to be like this:
As a magician makes illusions
Of horses, oxen, carts and other things,
Nothing is as it appears.

Buddha, born Siddhartha Gautama
(c. 450 BCE–c. 370 BCE)
from: *The Tibetan Book of Living and Dying*, Sogyal Rinpoche

1

Introduction: the mother of all misunderstandings

Confusion is the only suffering.
Confusion is when you argue with what is.
When you are perfectly clear, what is is what you want.
So when you want something that's different from what is,
you can know that you're very confused.

Byron Katie
from: A Thousand Names for Joy

There's something strange about the phenomenon of love: it can take us from the greatest heights of happiness, to the lowest depths of misery and pain. If perhaps, out of the blue, the person you've secretly admired for months has put their arms around you and kissed you, and said they've loved you from the start, then you've known amazing happiness. If you've ever laid in bed with your lover for hours, and dared to talk about and try all kinds of exciting fantasies, then you've experienced ecstasy. If you've been longing for years to have a baby, and one day you and your partner look at the pregnancy test and see that it's positive, then you've known profound joy.

But also, if the person who's starred in your fantasies for months falls into someone else's arms, then you've experienced the most agonising disappointment. And if the partner you've been with for years lies in bed with someone else for hours while you stay home and mind the children, then you've known excruciating pain. And when the divorce is final and you're living alone again, totally consumed by loneliness and despair, then you know the meaning of loneliness and despair.

In view of this profundity of both happiness and suffering, countless books have been written about love; most of them have been descriptive, admiring or critical, or in the form of a user guide on how to survive in this beautiful and dangerous jungle that we call love.

This book is about love and pain, but more about the part of us that feels love and suffers pain: the mind. Because we don't recognise the true nature of the mind, our understanding of the phenomenon of love is fundamentally flawed. And because of this, we create the painful misery that love is actually supposed to eliminate.

This book examines a misunderstanding that is so vast, so all-encompassing, so completely life-dominating, that I don't know where to start. After all, there might be aspects of it that have never consciously troubled you, and my explanation might seem to be talking a problem into existence. What's more, this misunderstanding depends on how one looks at it, so there are also many misunderstandings about the fundamental misunderstanding itself. Or to put it in more practical terms: a lot of people are very skilled at denying this problem, although in fact it causes many problems, which in turn serve as a further incentive to deny it. In short, this book is about the mother of all problems, which at first will perhaps require some effort to identify. But when you do, you'll experience a thrill of recognition... and then the fun will really begin!

The cause of this fundamental misunderstanding lies in our mind, and especially our relationship with ourselves, or more exactly, in the way we relate to and react to our own thoughts and emotions. This book is about the deeper layer of the mind where the cause of much suffering – both in and outside relationships – occurs. Learning to understand that cause won't be easy as it requires an open mind that is willing to conduct research before making judgement. Yet even just researching the reality behind the misunderstanding is more interesting and inspiring than simply remaining trapped in it. As you read this book, one can learn many new things about the mind, and learn to look at it in a completely different way. And the great thing is that you don't have to believe anything or accept anything on anyone else's authority. You can verify the accuracy of everything in this book, using practical exercises that it presents, which will help to develop a clear view of your mind and reality. In this book, the mind is simultaneously the researcher and the subject of the research. This research into the mind will inevitably lead you to a resolution of the misunderstanding, and hence to the real nature of yourself and all that exists. This reality is so incredibly profound, joyful, and obvious, that it's almost impossible to explain. But only almost!

I'd like to start by explaining how I became aware of this problem and its solution. After a life filled with both happiness and misery – including various love relationships, raising four children, quite a few addictions, a lot of hard work in several jobs, a massive burnout, a divorce, boring and interesting studies, and a variety of therapies and training courses – basically, after a very ordinary life, at the age of 45, I started to help people stop smoking. I had recently broken the habit myself, and was naturally delighted to have done so. I was also taking a course to become a qualified trainer, so it seemed a good idea to set up my own stop smoking course. This was an immediate success, and a year later I wrote a book on how to stop smoking (Dutch title *De opluchting*, published in the USA as *Quit Smoking in One Day*), which soon became a bestseller. The publicity resulting from this eventually led to requests for help with other addictions. Then I started to see a pattern in addiction problems: each was the consequence of striving for more happiness and less misery. But the very means used in attempting to become happier were causing the misery of addiction. The means used in the attempt to eliminate painful feelings were in fact multiplying those painful feelings.

When the effect of an action is precisely the opposite of what was intended, we call it a counterproductive reflex. A frequently cited example is scratching an itchy mosquito bite: it actually makes it itch more. An addiction is a classic example of a counterproductive reflex: the aim of the drug is to get rid of an oppressive feeling and create a good feeling instead; this works very briefly during each 'high', but at the same time, the use of the drug strengthens the negative feelings one was trying to escape. If you drink alcohol in order to lose your inhibitions with other people, you're going to feel increasingly inhibited and will increasingly need alcohol if you ever want to do anything spontaneous. If you use pep pills in order to overcome chronic fatigue and gain a more energetic approach to life, you're going to feel increasingly tired and eventually won't even be able to clean the house without the pep pills. In short, any apparent advantages of the drug turn out to be merely fleeting moments in a gradual downward slope towards more and more misery. The drug becomes increasingly necessary as a means to occasionally escape from that misery, at least briefly. I wrote about these findings in a book on addiction (Dutch title *De verslaving voorbij*, not yet published in English; the title translates as *Beyond Addiction*), and many people discovered that ending an addiction is much easier than it seems when you're still addicted, and even much more pleasant. In other words, the idea that it's extremely difficult to stop is an illusion created by the addiction itself. This fear of stopping is precisely the essence of being addicted. It's a self-fulfilling fear: the only thing sustained by a counterproductive reflex, such as an addiction, is itself. As soon as the addicted mind sees through its own misunderstanding, it is free. Then stopping turns out to be a joyful liberation and a relief: the opposite of what you – as an addict – were afraid of.

While working with addicts, it became clear to me that the negative feelings they were trying to eradicate by using drugs were acquired during their upbringing. I discovered that the way in which parents try to raise their children to become happy and successful adults actually gives them the belief that they're not good enough as they are, and need to learn how to fulfil countless conditions first. This creates in children a fundamental insecurity and self-rejection, which as adults they try to suppress at all costs, i.e. sometimes by using drugs. Here too, a counterproductive pattern is at work: the very way in which parents try to achieve their children's happiness in fact causes them the greatest misery in adult life. I wrote a book on this subject (Dutch title *Het einde van de opvoeding*, not yet published in English; the title translates as *The End of Parenting*), which gave me the opportunity to talk to parents about their problematic children. In most cases, I found that the child's 'problem' had been created – or at least exacerbated and sustained – by the parents, in the manner in which they were trying to resolve it! As soon as the parents understood this, and switched their focus from correcting the child to accepting themselves and their fear of not being good parents, the child's problem often immediately disappeared! The counterproductive nature of good intentions is thus always connected with fear: precisely by running away from that fear, we create the very consequences that we feared.

As a result of writing these books, I also received requests from readers to help in a relationship crisis. And yes, you guessed it, I found the same counterproductive reflex operating in relationship problems: the way partners try to save relationships actually increases their relationship misery, until a break-up is inevitable. And behind this mechanism there appears to be an even deeper and more astonishing reflex: precisely the way we strive for love and security intensifies our loneliness and dependence, and – if we ever have a chance to find happiness – causes us to unintentionally and unconsciously destroy that happiness. The way we strive to find and maintain a love relationship already carries the seeds of that relationship's failure, as well as the pain of loneliness and abandonment. And this deep pain that we feel when a relationship fails only strengthens the craving to find a new love relationship, or conversely, sometimes to avoid such relationships altogether. Either way, however, we again fall into the same trap and sow the seeds of the next painful crisis.

Once you've noticed it, you'll start to see this counterproductive reflex all the time in a whole host of smaller problems. The poses we adopt to hide our insecurity from strangers actually create more insecurity. Our little strategies for getting others to admire us actually intensify our lack of self-esteem. The white lies we tell to avoid rejection actually reinforce our fear of rejection. The tricks by which we try to retain or repeat pleasant feelings actually ruin the pleasure. The methods we use in the attempt to protect ourselves from distress actually create all kinds of suffering. In other words, every form of protection against emotional fear and pain gradually turns into oppression. Our whole identity, all the patterns and automatic responses we've acquired in order to function as a woman or man, as a mother or father, among friends or colleagues and even when we're alone, all those patterns result in precisely the opposite of what we're aiming for. We curtail or spoil our happiness by the way we cling to it. We increase or prolong our misery by the way we try to eradicate it. In the words of the Buddhist sage Shantideva (8th century CE):

Although wishing to be rid of misery,
(All beings) run towards misery itself.
Although wishing to have happiness,
Like an enemy they ignorantly destroy it.

This is the problem addressed by this book, and it's a rather stubborn and deep-rooted problem. The good news is, however, that it can be solved. After all, it's based on a misunderstanding, and on a merely self-sustaining one at that. It's a vicious misunderstanding: it arises time after time as a result of our reaction to the consequences of the previous misunderstanding. Time after time we create our suffering and destroy our happiness. This book will show you how you can stop this, how you can learn to do nothing instead of creating misery, how you can learn to give instead of continuing to feel want and neediness, how you can learn to embrace what you now condemn and reject. In short, you'll learn to recognise the patterns that come into play when you try to eradicate your negative feelings, which actually only lead to those negative feelings being repeatedly evoked. You'll see that happiness is much nearer than you ever imagined. You don't need to find that prince on the white horse, or that super sexy lover; you don't need to get rich, or find a fantastic job, or acquire a new house; you don't need to achieve that far-distant state of enlightenment before you can find this happiness. It's very close to home, and is found when you see through the fundamental misunderstanding and recognise the essence of your own mind. This will automatically lead you to let go of the causes of suffering and develop the skilful means that will lead you to unconditional happiness. You will then, and only then, be able to engage in truly loving relationships. And if you happen to get that fantastic job or that new house, then great – but your happiness will no longer depend on it.

So, is your life currently in a crisis? A relationship crisis? Or the opposite: a loneliness crisis? An identity crisis, burnout or depression? However painful that may be for you, it's actually a favourable circumstance for learning to recognise the entire self-sustaining crisis system, and breaking out of it for ever. But even if your life is currently running smoothly, and you have a good, loving relationship or are enjoying life to the full as a single person, that's OK too! You can still use this book to see how you're limiting your own happiness, and already creating future misery. And also learn how to stop doing that, and instead create happiness for yourself and others.

Because beyond the whole cycle of longing for love, finding love, losing love and anguishing over that loss, there's a state of being that is totally free from the desperate striving for love and approval, for the simple reason that this state of being is love itself. It's possible and practicable to liberate yourself from striving for love, by realising that this love has always been there, within yourself. In this state of being there is never again a want of love, the idea of needing love is inconceivable. It's an effortless state of unconditionally giving and receiving love. Really, it's possible. And now I'd very much like to explain how you can achieve it.

2

The first layer of our identity: the negative belief

All suffering is caused by our clinging to a wrong sense of self

Buddhist teaching

My first experience in the area of love was called Maartje, and occurred when I was in the first year of high school, aged eleven. The experience consisted of fantasising about her, gazing in deep melancholy at the class photo she was in, and nervously avoiding her proximity in class. The idea of actually saying anything to her was just too scary to imagine, and so it remained a secret love, which had an unhappy ending on the school trip to the Han Caves in Belgium just before the summer holidays that year. The class was walking through the dark subterranean tunnels, where weak light bulbs positioned at 50-metre intervals provided faint glimmers of illumination. I was walking behind Maartje, and next to her was one of the coolest guys in the class. As we walked, I saw they were holding hands. Each time we approached the dark section between two lights, their heads moved closer together, and when it got brighter again near the next light, they moved apart. I don't remember now whether I found it very painful to see this, but I do still remember that the movement of the two heads towards and away from each other seemed to be almost mechanically controlled by the changing light level in the tunnel. Presumably, I was already repressing painful feelings with a rational observation. In any event, this love didn't last very long after that.

Anyone who's been through one of those tender adolescent infatuations will recall the intensity of fear and hope: fear that your feelings will be discovered and ridiculed, and hope that they will be reciprocated. In this interplay of hope and fear, the stakes are high: total rejection versus complete acceptance. And if you don't dare to join in the game, and keep your feelings a secret, the result is frustration and self-rejection. In short, the whole situation surrounding infatuation seems to mainly derive its incredibly high level of tension from the chance of both absolute acceptance and utter rejection.

While this tension is clearly visible in adolescent infatuation, it also continues to operate in later and more 'adult' forms of amorous longing, though often in a covert form. For example, the man who tells his new girlfriend about his earlier love adventures, but fails to mention his occasional visits to a sex worker, is giving in to his fear of rejection. And the woman who tells her husband that she'd like to go on holiday without him sometime will be afraid of his rejection. If you look closely at your own behaviour, you'll see that in both the initial phase of a relationship and the subsequent stable phase you're almost constantly trapped in this interplay of hope and fear. Not that you constantly feel hope and fear; especially in the stable phase of a relationship, you're usually so accustomed to the situation and to your partner that you can successfully steer clear of those feelings. You already know what behaviour is best avoided and what behaviour will almost certainly result in praise, and as far as possible you live within these safe paths of preventing rejection and generating praise. It requires open, honest self-analysis to discover these mechanisms within yourself, but they're always there, even when you think you have 'a good relationship'.

That we keep to these fear-avoiding paths is manifested most clearly in the interaction with a lover, although we do it with everyone. The strength of the hope and fear, however, is proportionate to the intensity of your feelings for someone, so you'll generally find this much less of a problem at the baker's shop, for instance. But if you've waited for a considerable amount of time, and it's nearly your turn, then a customer who just walked in is served before you, then the interplay of hope and fear immediately jolts into action. You hope your rights will be respected and you fear rejection. Not expressing your anger for the sake of peace and quiet usually makes you feel as if you're weak, which is a form of self-rejection. So we're caught in a dilemma of hope for respect and fear of rejection on the one hand, and self-rejection on the other.

The cause of this fundamental hope and fear lies in the nature of our relationship with ourselves, i.e. our self-image, our identity; and the structure of this is entirely determined by self-rejection. In the chapters that follow, I will first explain this structure of our self-image, plus some other counterproductive mechanisms that we use in our quest for happiness and approval. See also Figure 1 on page 7. After that, I will illustrate how these mechanisms mean that love relationships are mostly destined to fail, because they create the very misery that we're trying to escape by engaging in such relationships. The second half of the book then deals with how we can let go of these counterproductive mechanisms, and how we can live – with or without a relationship – in love and independence.

The core of our self-image is self-rejection and aversion to self-rejection, which I summarise with the term 'the negative belief'. I call it a belief because it isn't true, and negative because it causes suffering. No one is born with a negative belief, yet everyone has one. We learn it during the first ten years of life. If you observe babies and very young infants, you see that they have no image of themselves at all, and therefore, no negative or self-rejecting image. Their behaviour is uninhibited and spontaneous: when they're angry, they yell; when they're hungry, they cry; when they're happy, they shout with joy. This natural, spontaneous behaviour of small children is sometimes regarded as a higher state of being, a natural state of being that we, as adults, have lost and need to find again. This is a misunderstanding. The natural state of small children is not a 'higher state of being', for the simple reason that the child is not actually aware of it. Children are at the mercy of their own spontaneity, and this can also make them feel very unsafe, powerless and frustrated.

These very young children are thus in a pre-self-image stage, but when they reach the age of about one year to eighteen months, a mental self-image starts to develop, at about the same time as the first language development, and also the parents' first attempts to set limits for the child's behaviour. As soon as parents notice that functional communication with the child is becoming possible, the actual 'parenting' starts: attempts to teach the child to do certain things and to stop doing others, in her/his future interest. The child perceives (at first unconsciously) that she is no longer unconditionally admired, cherished and cared for, as in the womb and during the first year of life, but needs to change her behaviour to make sure she continues to get that care and praise. Emptying the bottle results in being praised, not emptying it results in feeling the mother's anxiety. Peeing in the potty is a great success, but peeing somewhere near the potty increasingly causes disapproval. Running around the house singing in the middle of the night might seem funny when you're very young, but if a four-year-old does it, most parents aren't amused. But this is not a mistake on the part of the parents; on the contrary, it's very normal to gradually set limits for the child's behaviour, otherwise she wouldn't develop any language or self-image at all. There are well-known cases of children being raised by animals, or locked up by a psychotic mother and only given food, with no further contact. These children grew up like animals, with no language skills or self-reflection. This is another indication that small children, in the same way as animals, are not at a higher state of being, even though they live in the 'here and now'. The formation of an ego or self-image is evidently a necessary step in human development, and only after this is it possible for spiritual development beyond the ego to take place.

A child's first moments of 'self-consciousness' arise when the initial unconditional and total acceptance comes to an end, and the rejection and correction of undesirable behaviour begins. The child learns that she's not good enough as she is, and needs to fulfil certain conditions in order to feel that she's good or wanted. So although this is a very normal developmental process, we should not underestimate the deep fears that can be involved for the child. The deep feelings of dependency that we can sometimes feel as adults, for instance when a love relationship breaks down, originate in this initial stage of our upbringing. In an adult they are in fact illusory, they don't correspond with reality. Adults can, after all, take care of themselves, however strong the 'I can't live without you' feeling might be. But for a small child, the feeling of dependency does indeed correspond with reality. If you can't walk, can't do anything with your hands, can't talk, have no money or house or other possessions, then you're really very dependent on your mother's kindness. So if she's angry because you didn't empty your bottle or missed the potty when you peed, then the fear that this evokes is actually related to true dependency. For the same reason, children who had a difficult or premature birth or insecure early childhood show an above-average tendency to suffer from anxiety disorders in adulthood.

We all spent our first years of life in a state of true dependency and existential fear of rejection. That fear is thus originally a fear of abandonment, and in essence a fear of death. Therefore, it is no wonder that we have this fear for the rest of our lives, and try our best to keep it hidden. Fear is the deepest force behind our lifelong striving to gain the love and approval of others.

Is it now clear that our negative belief, our deepest feeling of not being good enough, is the basis of our self-image and hence love relationships? This is not a denial of the beautiful and loving aspects that are also part of most relationships. It's a starting point from where you can identify and solve your present and future relationship problems. Think about the relationship crises you've experienced in your life. Try to feel that misery again, that distress, that fear of losing the other person, that excruciating hope and uncertainty about whether they really want you. Observe the agonising feeling of need, of the inability to live without them, the frustrating powerlessness, the feelings of failure and weakness, of guilt and reproach. If you analyse those feelings carefully, you'll see that within the pain, all sense of self-esteem disappears. That is the negative belief, your deepest self-rejection.

The negative belief is therefore not the rational view that you have of yourself as an adult. You probably know quite well that you're not completely worthless, that you're good at sports, or intelligent, cultured, polite and socially sensitive, that you can love, and can take care of your loved ones. But when your lover abandons you, or you've been alone without love and approval for too long, then that feeling of being worthless can suddenly be activated; the feeling of fear, inferiority and failure. At that moment, the knowledge that you're probably quite a good, kind person is of no help whatsoever, because the feeling of self-rejection is simply much stronger. That is your negative belief and the core of your self-image.

It's very important that you learn to name this negative belief. You don't need to learn what it feels like: you know that already, you've felt it often enough in your life – or at least felt the fear of feeling it – so you know what we're talking about. But you've also always tried very hard to run away from it, to keep it covered with the other aspects of your self-image, so it's a good idea to stop running away from it, and start focusing your attention on it. Think back to crises in your life, to times of abandonment and loneliness, or when you lost something very precious, or when something very important went wrong. Try to describe that deep, self-rejecting feeling in a few words. A list of the most common descriptions of the negative belief is given below. Perhaps you'll find one or more that match the way you sometimes reject yourself. If not, then start by crossing out all the descriptions that couldn't possibly apply. When you've found one or more that matches, reflect for a while on the idea that this is your deepest belief about yourself, even when you're not feeling it.

I am worthless
I am stupid
I am pathetic
I am weak

I am bad
I am selfish
I am insignificant
I am ordinary
I am not good enough
I am a failure
I am a loser
I am dull
I am mediocre
I am cowardly
I am lazy
I am nothing
I am odd
I am ugly
I am inferior
I have no right to exist
I don't matter
I don't fit in
I am a nuisance

Have you found one or more? Well done! This is the illusory basis of your illusory identity. The term 'illusory' does not mean, however, that the resulting misery doesn't feel very real. It just means that it doesn't bear any relation to what you really are, only to what you've learned to believe you are.

Now that you've found the basis of your identity, I suggest that you do the mirror test and turn this possibly interesting theory into an actual experience. I mentioned this test in my previous books, and have received many remarkable responses from readers. I will give an explanation of the mirror test later in this book, but you must have already done it before then.

This is the mirror test: stand in front of a reasonably large mirror. Make sure you're alone and can't be disturbed. Look at your mirror image, with no positive or negative intentions, i.e. as neutrally as possible. And then say your negative belief out loud, without introduction or explanation, without mitigation or condemnation, without understatement or exaggeration, without any other words around it, just as if it were a simple fact: I am stupid, I am worthless, I am weak, or whatever your negative belief is. And then look carefully at both your mirror image and your inner world. Just give it a try; don't miss this opportunity for an extraordinary experience! After you've done this, stay focused on yourself for a while, in a quiet place where you're alone and feel comfortable. Good luck!

3

The second layer of our identity: the basic rules

Everything is an illusion except goodness

Buddhist saying

The core of our identity is thus negative belief, our self-rejection. It is because of this self-rejection that our true nature – which is perfect in itself – remains invisible to us, and we get ensnared in negative assumptions about ourselves. This is the first layer of the veil that covers our natural state of being (see Figure 1 on page 7). But it's a painful and fearful veil, and we have a strong aversion to it. This gives rise to the rest of our identity, which serves to cover the painful self-rejection, so we don't feel it. And this is where denial of the denial begins: we no longer remember that there's a natural state from which we've become alienated, we just want to stop the painful feeling of inadequacy and worthlessness.

The first layer of our identity, the negative belief, then becomes covered by a second layer. This consists of all the basic rules and conditions that we must fulfil in order to feel that we're good and worthwhile. Fulfilling these conditions gains the love and approval of others, and avoids rejection. The first rules that we learn are the usual conditions imposed in parenting: you must be good, you mustn't be naughty, you must do what you're told, you mustn't get angry, you must be nice, you must do your best, you mustn't be lazy, you must get good results, you mustn't lie, you must be honest, you must be strong, you mustn't be weak, and so on. Most of these rules continue to apply throughout your life, and new ones are added as the years go by. For instance, in adolescence: you must be sexy, you mustn't be nerdy, you must fit in, you must be cool, you mustn't try too hard. Then yet more rules for adults: you must be successful, you must earn more money, you must have an interesting job, you must have a healthy lifestyle, you must have a good relationship, you must be socially sensitive, you mustn't fail, you mustn't be selfish, you mustn't be indecisive, and so on.

Perhaps you'll say that many of these rules are actually true, that surely it's better not to be selfish, and to be socially sensitive. Yes certainly, of course it is; but if we're faced with the choice of obeying one of these excellent rules or avoiding a possible rejection, then we usually choose the latter. Consider the following example: you're in the lift with a colleague, you politely say 'Good morning' to each other, and you notice that he has very bad breath. Both the rule that you must be honest and the rule that you must be socially sensitive dictate here that you should discreetly alert him to the problem, so that he can do something about it, and other colleagues and clients will be spared the unpleasantness. Yet, in this situation most people will say nothing, since their fear of rejection by that colleague takes precedence over those rules – naturally very worthy in themselves – of honesty and social sensitivity. Some people will perhaps be restrained not so much by the fear of rejection, but by the fear that the other person will feel rejected. However, this is a projection of your own fear of rejection. Think about it: why would you feel bad if the other person felt rejected? Because you'd feel guilty about it, and that is a form of self-rejection. The phenomenon of projection will be explained in more detail in Chapter 8.

This is not to suggest, of course, that fear of rejection is the only motivation behind what we do in life. We naturally also have authentic, altruistic motives. I want to make clear that the fear of rejection is a kind of filter through which all other motives pass. Regardless of how altruistic an intended action might be, if it also arouses a fear of rejection, people will usually choose the safe option to avoid the risk of rejection. The need for an altruistic action can still be fulfilled in a different way.

So how does this second layer of our identity operate? Well, as long as we obey all the rules that we've learned, there's no problem. As long as we're good, do our best, don't do bad things, help others, are kind to others, we feel relatively safe from rejection and self-rejection. However, as soon as we break one or more of these rules, or even think about it, an inner voice warns us, and threatens us with rejection. This voice is sometimes called our inner judge or inner critic, and in some psychological approaches, the superego. If we think of this second layer of basic rules as the law that we must obey, then the inner voice is the judge or the police who enforce that law. The punishment threatened by the judge is our negative belief: if you fail to comply with this condition, then you're going to feel worthless. If you don't stand up for yourself (when someone pushes in front of you at the bakery), then you're a weakling. If you tell your colleague he has bad breath, he's going to feel very hurt, and you'll be an ill-mannered oaf who goes around offending people.

In this way, our inner judge keeps us on the right path. The right path? No, the safe path, the path that gives the lowest risk of rejection by others or of self-rejection. But exactly how safe is this path? Imagine that you're at a party, and you're feeling fine. Suddenly you have the idea of singing a song you wrote yourself, in front of everyone. You hesitate, and then the inner judge kicks in and threatens you with the self-rejection of being a show-off who wants to be the centre of attention. Or threatens you with other people's rejection: they'll laugh at you or, even worse, completely ignore you. You sigh, have another glass of wine, and decide to give up on the idea. So is your peace of mind restored? Absolutely not, because now your inner judge pronounces another opinion: 'What a coward, why can't you just be spontaneous for once?' In short, it's become a no-win situation: whatever you do, there's (fear of) rejection. This is because the basic rules in the second layer of our identity are not consistent with each other. For instance, here are a few of those opposite – or apparently opposite – rules:

I must be strong	/ I must show vulnerability
I must be a leader	/ I must be modest
I must give an intelligent answer	/ I mustn't be arrogant
I must be assertive	/ I must be nice
I must be spontaneous	/ I must keep control of myself
I must be independent	/ I must bond with other people
I must protect my freedom	/ I must dare to make commitments
I must be healthy	/ I must enjoy life
I mustn't lie	/ I mustn't hurt other people
I must help other people	/ I must respect everyone's privacy

Do you notice anything about these opposites? The rules in the first column are mainly aimed at avoiding self-rejection, while the rules in the second column are mainly aimed at avoiding other people's rejection. If you lie, you feel worthless; but if you're honest and consequently hurt someone, that person will reject you. What you're actually afraid of in that case is feeling worthless if the other person rejects you or feels hurt. So that fear too is actually fear of the risk of self-rejection, but at a deeper level.

For example, if you see that someone is sad, you might feel the need to comfort them or offer help. But at the same time you feel slightly afraid that the other person will be embarrassed by your attention. So there's both a spontaneous need to express yourself, and the fear that the other person will reject your spontaneous expression. In this way, the second layer of our identity creates a tension, which makes it almost impossible for us to be carefree. We must always be on our guard to avoid (self-)rejection. This is a completely hopeless endeavour: if we do something, there's fear of rejection; if we don't do it, there's self-rejection. Every time we successfully avoid the one (rejection by others), we sustain and even reinforce the other (self-rejection). Once we're on the path of avoidance, we must constantly comply with these contradictory rules in the second layer of our identity.

It's just like when you have a secret lover: every day that you don't tell your partner makes it more difficult to say anything about it the next day. After the first lie, you're committed to that path and the lies stack up, one on top of another. It's the fear of rejection and loss of self-esteem that forces us to maintain that artificial identity. It's like an addiction: once you start using a drug to suppress your negative feelings, you become increasingly dependent on it and must continue taking it, otherwise you'll feel even worse about yourself. And you're also going to feel increasingly bad about that dependency. Taking the drug or abstaining from it causes more negative feelings. That is an addiction: a problem that's made worse by our chosen 'solution' for it. The most fundamental problem is our belief in our own inadequacy and worthlessness. Our 'solution' is to construct a positive self-image on the basis of other people's love and approval. This constructed self-image, also known as the 'ego', is our most fundamental addiction. Artificial self-esteem is the high that we're chasing. Other people's love and approval are the drugs that we can't live without, and will do anything to get.

The second layer of our identity constitutes a reversal of the direction in which the mind looks: because of the convincing illusion of worthlessness, of not being good enough, of being stupid, weak or bad, the mind turns away from its own nature and looks outward, to other people, in the first place naturally the parents. They now become the suppliers of safety, love and approval, and the child's mind is only too happy to deny itself and please the other person, in exchange for that protection from fear and self-rejection. However, this is ironic: this self-denial only reinforces the illusion. Running away from the painful illusion of worthlessness and dependence gives it an ever-greater semblance of reality; the fear of it confirms its existence. Every time we yield to that inner judge, that internalised voice of our parents and educators, we forfeit our autonomy, and lose our natural and spontaneous state. In Buddhism this situation is explained with the following example:

Imagine that you arrive home at dusk, and see a venomous snake in the corner of the room. In reality it is not a snake at all, but a piece of rope carelessly left lying around, which you mistake for a snake. In panic, you run outside and slam the door shut behind you. You never dare to go back into the house again. That is what our existential situation is like.

The main character in this example actually makes three mistakes, each of which causes misery to an increasing extent. The first mistake is not recognising the piece of rope as a piece of rope. This is our ignorance of who or what we really are, our natural state of being. The second mistake is seeing a dangerous snake. This is our misconception that we are fundamentally flawed, stupid, weak or bad, and not good enough; in short: worthless. The third mistake is acting on the fear of the snake and running outside. This is running away from our negative feelings about ourselves, and looking for other people's love and approval. This is the most serious mistake, because it makes it impossible to see through the other mistakes. As long as we keep looking for other people's love and approval, we sustain the illusion that without that love we're worthless, not good enough, which in turn reinforces the urge to look for that approval outside ourselves. It's a vicious circle, and the main cause of all other counterproductive reflexes in our life. Like the person in India who lived the rest of her life in the garden for fear of the supposed snake in the house, we're also alienated from ourselves, we daren't come home to ourselves, for fear of our supposed worthlessness and inadequacy. These negative feelings are not really true, they don't relate to what we are in reality, but only to what we've learned to think about ourselves.

Our real or natural state is perfect in itself, overflowing with love and goodness. It radiates qualities such as honesty, strength, spontaneity, creativity, compassion, and many more. Perhaps you see this as wishful thinking, as a positive belief instead of a negative one? In essence, it's not; I will give reasons for this assertion later in the book. At this stage, however, it's better to first be well-acquainted with the mistake, before undergoing a detailed analysis of the reality behind it. Otherwise you could indeed fall into that New Age trap, and turn reality – your own fundamental goodness – into a positive belief, as the umpteenth means of covering your negative belief. That won't help you much, and is more likely to hinder you from discovering your natural state. You see: if you *believe* that you're fundamentally good, this might help you to sometimes feel better. But each time you feel worthless again, this positive belief will seriously turn against you and reinforce your self-rejection. It's only when you *realise* your perfect, natural state – your real state of being beyond self-rejection – that it becomes resistant to negative feelings. And until then, your mind won't recognise its own nature; it will think instead that it sees an imperfect nature, an inadequate, inferior essence, and will turn away from itself in order to escape that painful notion, and seek other people for the love and safety that it thinks it lacks. This in turn maintains the belief in its own negative nature. Can you see that this has both a tragic side and a humorous side? It's tragic as long as we're completely caught in this self-created impasse. But then the funny side becomes apparent when we start to figure out that it's just a misunderstanding.

Another analogy from Buddhism is that of a beggar who lives in an old hut and has to beg for sustenance every day, not knowing that an enormous chest of gold is buried underneath his hut. Isn't that very tragic until he discovers the chest of gold? Then it becomes funny, right? It's the same in this book: first you're shown all the misery you've being trying to escape all your life, and then you see that it's a gigantic mistake, a joke on a cosmic scale that got completely out of hand; but all the funnier once you get it! So hang in there, lots more surprises are on the way!

4

The third layer of our identity: patterns in thinking, feeling and behaviour

Of all affectations, none is weightier than your 'you-ness':
When you are occupied with your own self, you are separated from truth.

Abu Sa'id, Sufi master
(967-1049)

In the last chapter I described the second layer of our identity, consisting of basic rules and conditions, which is characterised by the mind turning away from its own supposedly inadequate nature and looking for happiness and safety outside itself. The consequence of this reversal of focus is manifested in the third layer of our identity: here the mind has lost contact with itself, and lives in a make-believe world of automatic responses and projections.

As we saw earlier, the misconception that we're not good enough, in combination with the reflex to run away from this unpleasant feeling, sustains itself and forms the basis of all our counterproductive reflexes. In childhood we constantly learn solutions for both major and minor fears of rejection, all strategies to avoid fears and gain approval. This is based on the need for self-protection, not only from rejection, but also from the fear of rejection. This self-protection is achieved by learning to avoid or suppress behaviour that has previously been rejected by other people. When the toddler in muddy shoes jumps around on the lovely white IKEA lounge suite, singing and dancing for the sheer joy of life, and then gets an angry response from her mother, she's probably going to feel rejected. Not only the muddy shoes, but also the spontaneous uprush of joie de vivre will now be associated with rejection. In future, she will be inclined to choose the safe path and suppress spontaneous impulses. Thus the child learns to mistrust and suppress spontaneous expressions of the natural state, in order to avoid rejection. So you see: safety and self-protection are basically forms of self-rejection.

I should mention, however, that here we're only talking about safety in the sense of protection from rejection. There's nothing wrong with protecting your child from physical dangers, for instance, when crossing a busy street. However, the way parents sometimes do this can contribute to the child's self-rejection. I was recently cycling behind a nervous mother who was cycling next to her three year-old daughter. At first the little girl seemed to be enjoying her recently acquired cycling skills. But during the hundred yards that I cycled behind them, she received a non-stop torrent of urgent warnings and harsh criticism from her mother, with a jittery undercurrent of fear and tension. What the child is learning is not only how to ride a bike, but also to feel just as frightened and uncertain about herself as her mother. This constant anxiety about horrible accidents is one of those automatic mental responses that creates misery through the way one tries to avoid misery. To reiterate: it's completely fine to protect your child from physical distress; the misery only arises when this is done on the basis of fear and the anticipated guilt and self-reproach if something were to actually go wrong.

The third layer of our identity contains a rich diversity of mechanisms intended to keep us from being rejected. One of these is the 'nice guy' pattern, and I am personally an example of this. I am the youngest of six children and also an 'afterthought': my brother and four sisters were between five and ten years older. One of the negative beliefs about myself that I acquired in childhood is 'I am weak'. And when I was a small child, this was actually true: compared with the others, I had very little to contribute, because other family members were much stronger. I remember being furious with one of my sisters because she'd wrongly accused me of something, and she just fell about laughing at me. Finding it so hilarious, she even shouted to the others: 'Hey guys, come and look, little Jan's lost his temper!' That made me feel so powerless and rejected, that the rule 'you mustn't get angry' was immediately created in the second layer of my identity. The resulting pattern in the third layer is to be nice and avoid conflicts. If I sense the slightest threat of a confrontation and feel that I'm getting even slightly angry, I immediately smile and put on my most reassuring expression. As you might expect, I always chose the 'peaceful' solution at the bakery, and said nothing if someone pushed in front of me. Or if I saw someone make a mistake, I would instantly hasten to explain it away, so they wouldn't think I was being critical. 'Sorry for existing, I won't be a nuisance' is the actual meaning of the 'nice guy' pattern. Of course, it doesn't especially enhance your self-esteem, but it does enhance your fear of confrontation, which makes it a vicious and self-sustaining pattern. It becomes increasingly essential to put on the show of niceness in order to conceal your feelings of fear and weakness. This causes it to become like an addiction: it makes you feel worthless, but the fear of stopping is too great. The second part of this book deals with how you can let go of such restrictive patterns in your identity.

Another example of a possible pattern in the third layer of identity is perfectionism. On the basis of the negative belief 'I am not good enough', a rule has arisen in the second layer: 'you must be successful', 'you mustn't make any mistakes', or something like 'you're only as good as your results'. This gives rise to a compulsive pattern of perfectionism, an inability to stop working on a task if the result isn't the best possible. This compulsion is nurtured by hope of approval and fear of failure. When a task is finished, there will perhaps be satisfaction and approval for a short time, but very soon doubts will start: 'Was it really alright? Could it not have been better? Those people who were so pleased don't know what they're talking about as a real expert would see that it's rubbish'. In short, the feeling that your results aren't good enough so you're not good enough will re-enter through the back door. And this is the feeling you were trying to cover with perfectionism.

On the basis of the same negative belief, however, a completely different rule can be established in the second layer: 'there's no point in doing your best', which gives rise in the third layer to a pattern of passivity, of putting off doing things and not finishing what you started. The strategy of this pattern is simple: because the results will never be good enough anyway, it's better to avoid achieving any results at all. In this way, you can at least avoid failing every time. It's evident that here too the solution is at least as bad as the problem, and ultimately the solution actually *is* the problem. Avoiding the fear of failure through procrastination and not doing things only reinforces the feeling that you're not good enough.

Another example: the negative belief 'I am worthless, I don't matter' can lead to a rule in the second layer that says: 'you must make yourself useful', which can give rise in the third layer to the pattern known as the 'helpaholic'. People with this pattern must always be there to help, and have a strong desire to be needed and indispensable. On the surface, this can seem rather like altruism, which is a natural quality. But there's a significant difference: a helpaholic can't say no, while an altruist can. Altruism springs from natural self-esteem, while a helpaholic tries to maintain his artificial self-esteem by being helpful. Thus the helpaholic is in fact mainly furthering his own ends, and often shuts himself off from other people's gratitude. The ultimate effect of his assistance is a feeling of emptiness and worthlessness, of not being appreciated and not mattering. That is to say: the same feeling he was trying to escape with his helpful behaviour.

I could give many other examples of third-layer patterns of this kind, and in the rest of the book you'll encounter several more. For now, however, it's important to see the general mechanism: fear is the cause, getting stuck in a pattern is the effect. All patterns arise from our fear of rejection, and the result is always more self-rejection. Every self-protective pattern thus ensures its own continued necessity. Once you've developed a strategy for getting other people's approval, simply the thought of letting go of this pattern will cause fear of rejection. And each time the strategy fails and you don't receive approval, or are rejected, deep feelings of worthlessness and failure immediately return. Which makes us try even harder, or conversely give up in desperation on all attempts to gain approval, and fall into a protracted period of entrapment in a negative self-image. A crisis like this can sometimes lead to addiction, or depression, or even suicide. You see: it's such a painful vicious circle, so understandable and so unnecessary! When you look at other people and yourself in this way, constantly going around on the carousel of fundamental misunderstanding and the attempt to escape from it, don't you feel your heart melt a little?

5

The fourth and final layer of our identity: the image

Who would you be without the thought that you should impress?

Byron Katie

Our mind's first misunderstanding is not recognising its own pure, perfect nature. Instead we think our nature is imperfect: dependent, weak, stupid, pathetic, or bad; in short, we develop an exceptionally painful negative belief about ourselves (the first layer of our identity). Our reaction to this – aversion to the negative belief – takes us even further away from home: we try to get rid of the feeling of worthlessness via other people's love and approval. At best, this works for a very short time, as afterwards the negative belief and the aversion to it only increases. We then learn lots of rules that point to getting other people's love and approval (the second layer of our identity), and develop a whole range of automatic responses and patterns – or tricks – aimed at capturing that love and approval (the third layer).

This entire layered construction, which we regard as our 'self', is by definition unstable. There are two reasons for this: first, it's not based on reality but on an illusion, i.e. the negative belief. Second, the layers with which we cover that illusion are as transient as feelings: every day and every hour they must be renewed, otherwise the self-rejection will soon show through again. Think about it, it's quite obvious: how long does a new car make you feel like you're a success in life? After a couple of months the effect wears off. How long do you feel appreciated after your manager's given you a compliment? If you don't hear anything more from him in a couple of weeks, or still haven't been promoted after a couple of years, you'll start to doubt yourself. How long do you feel loved after having wonderful sex with your lover? If she's not interested again for a couple of weeks, or maybe a couple of months, you'll start to doubt yourself. How long do you feel good when you're completely alone and have nothing to do? After a few minutes or perhaps a quarter of an hour you'll phone someone or turn the TV on. In short, once we've developed a negative self-image, and made our happiness dependent on other people's approval, we have to constantly put energy into sustaining this externally derived self-esteem. This is why our 'self-worth' doesn't give permanent security, but rather a fundamental feeling of insecurity. In order to deny that insecurity, and give the unstable 'self' construction some semblance of stability, we cloak it in a fourth layer: the image.

The image is how we want other people to see us. It's an idealised construction that's intended to create an appearance of self-confidence. It's the screen that stops other people from seeing our internal tangle of fears and cover-ups of fears. It's the outermost layer of our identity, which ensures that others see us as we'd like to see ourselves, and others don't see what we feel insecure about. It's the big 'I have got it all together' show that everyone puts on, all day, every day. Take a look at the image tricks that you use yourself. Here are a few questions to get your self-analysis started. If a new friend or love interest is coming to visit, do you look critically around your room to check that it's not too untidy (or conversely not too tidy)? Perhaps you put that very interesting book in a prominent place on the coffee table, because you want the other person to know that you read such high-minded literature? Or shove the trashy novel to the back of the bookcase because you're rather embarrassed about liking that kind of rubbish? Do you check that your hair's tidy (or – if you cultivate a youthful, casual image – that it's sufficiently untidy)? These are all aspects of your image. And when you're with people, especially those you don't know very well, what impression do you hope to make? The friendly, self-confident professional? The strong, energetic go-getter? The astute and beautiful business woman? The kind, comforting, and generous hostess?

And now look at other people from this angle, see the images they use. Sit for a while at an outdoor cafe and watch all the funny, beautiful images that go past: the scruffy nerd, the super-chic lady with her lapdog, the workman with a pencil behind his ear, the glamorous granny, the smooth businessman, the giggling group of young girls, the perfect son-in-law, the homeless man in badly fitting clothes, the sexy young woman; the list is endless. And again analyse carefully what appearance you choose and what impression you try to make on others. What clothes you most like to wear in public, what behaviour you usually employ in a new situation with people you don't know, for instance at a reception. Are you the good mixer who's never alone? Or the shy observer who pretends to gaze in fascination at a woodcut on the wall, glass of wine in hand? And when you're with friends, are you the talker or the listener? Do you go into questions in greater depth or do you simply brush problems aside? Do you prefer to lead or to follow? Do you talk about your experiences or would you rather hear about other people's? But be careful: don't reject yourself when you do this self-analysis. You don't need to change anything about yourself. Just look at what you do, with humour and without judgement. If you try to suppress your image, you only create a new one, such as the spiritually developed person who no longer needs an image. An image of egolessness is a contradiction in terms, and can only cause you a lot of misery.

Our identity or ego is therefore not a singular thing, but is composed of various layers that depend on and reinforce one another. There's no law that determines which negative belief leads to which basic rules, and how these in turn lead to a certain pattern and image. For instance, the negative belief 'I am stupid' can give rise to the basic rule 'learning is very important', with the behaviour pattern of the eager beaver student who tries to avoid the teacher's rejection.

Someone like this can then develop an image of the know-all or bookworm. But it's equally possible that the same negative belief can give rise to the basic rule 'you must have practical skills', with the behaviour pattern of seeking approval as a problem-solver. Someone like this then develops the handyman image. The owner of a hobby shop where I used to buy things would say to every customer as they paid, 'So, that's another problem solved'. He really enjoyed his work, unless you wanted something he didn't have in stock; that was clearly a source of great pain to him.

Finally, the very same belief 'I am stupid' can give rise to the basic rule 'studying is for suckers', which results in a behaviour pattern of resistance to every situation where you might be regarded as stupid. This goes well with the image of the rebel who rejects all established opinions. But the image of the rebel can also arise from a completely different negative belief, such as 'I am weak', plus the basic rule 'you must be smarter than the rest to get what you want', and a behaviour pattern of trickery.

Countless factors influence the development of the various layers of our identity. The most important are, naturally, the identities of our parents and educators. Other important influences are the social environment, the composition of the family unit and the extended family, specific traumatic experiences in childhood, the nature of the relationship between parents, the atmosphere at school, and so on. However, all these influences follow the same basic pattern:

1. Rejection of our natural, perfect qualities creates an illusion of inadequacy, a painful negative belief about ourselves.
2. We run away from this by obeying rules that give us other people's approval, or at least prevent other people's rejection.
3. This gives rise to innumerable patterns of thinking, feeling, and behaviour that we use, sometimes consciously but usually unconsciously, in order to capture love and approval and avoid rejection.
4. The image is actually one of those many behaviour patterns, but it also serves to conceal – from others and from yourself – the exis-

tence of other patterns and automatic responses, and how uncertain you feel about their functioning.

Figure 2 below is a diagram showing how (self-)rejection transforms our natural qualities into ego patterns. The centre of the diagram is the natural state of being, which radiates spontaneous expressions of honesty, gentleness, goodness, creativity, and so on. The bold

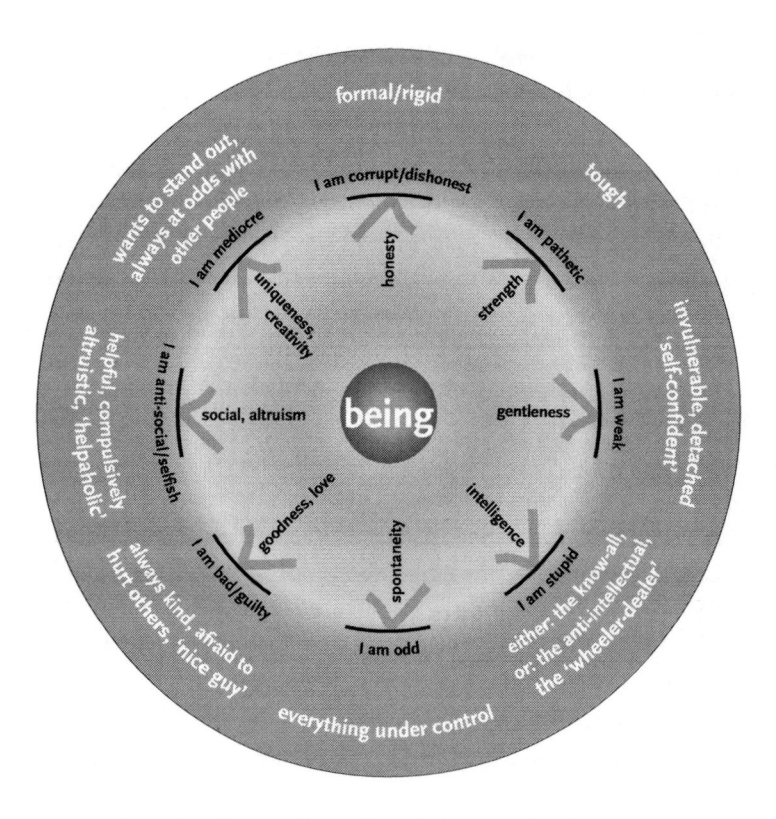

Figure 2: Natural qualities are distorted by rejection and self-rejection into ego patterns (from: Beyond Addiction).

lines around this area symbolise the rejection or blocking of these spontaneous expressions. In the zone outside these lines are negative beliefs that can result from this rejection. This is the zone of self-rejection. Around this is the (self)image that serves to conceal the negative belief. A few possible examples of the image are shown in white letters. The diagram is not intended to present a complete picture: these are classic examples that are sometimes found in practice.

6

Disruptions in the development of our identity

> *How sad that people ignore the near*
> *And search for truth afar:*
> *Like someone in the midst of water*
> *Crying out in thirst,*
> *Like a child of a wealthy home*
> *Wandering among the poor.*
>
> Hakuin Ekaku, Zen master
(1685-1768)

Describing our identity as an accumulation of layers, each one covering the ones below, could give the impression that its development is a purely chronological process. However, that is not the case. We don't first develop a negative belief, then construct a set of rules and conditions that must be fulfilled in order to obtain love and approval, and only then develop the behaviour patterns, and finally the image. It sometimes seems to be like this because as children get older they gradually lose their natural spontaneity, in exchange for an increasingly solid self-image. But in reality the four layers of the identity arise simultaneously, and only the solidity of the entire ego construction increases during childhood and reaches its adult level during adolescence. Young children can also lapse into ego behaviour if they feel afraid of rejection, want to fit in, or sweet-talk or whine in order to get their own way. But afterwards it's very easy for them to forget themselves again and become engrossed in the present moment's play. It's only in adolescence that the circle of self-rejection and fear of rejection appears to close, and the identification with the self-image becomes complete and permanent. Doesn't it sometimes just break your heart to see how absolutely and unashamedly adolescents surrender themselves to other people's approval for their self-esteem? They're like mirrors, perfectly reflecting the trend of the day: if the fashion among their friends is to have short hair and baggy jeans, then short hair and baggy jeans is what they must have. If the fashion is long hair and tight jeans, then they must have long hair and tight jeans, or they're going to feel stupid and worthless.

But please don't imagine that after our adolescent years we've become much wiser; we've only become somewhat more adroit at avoiding bitter disappointments. We're still fully focused on getting other people's approval, it's just that on average we're a bit more successful at it than adolescents, a bit smarter at evading the deepest pitfalls, and a bit more confident in our strategies for winning praise. And above all, we've developed an ever better image that hides how dependent we are on approval. It presents a picture of the autonomous, self-confident man or woman of the world, a picture that's so convincing that we often believe it ourselves. Until we lose that wonderful job, our partner leaves us, or we make that terrible mistake that hurts other people. Then it's back in an instant: that deep feeling of weakness, worthlessness, failure, or whatever your negative belief might be.

Although we can describe the history of our ego's development, the mental construction of the ego is repeated every single moment. The ego is a reaction, a self-protection reflex. Each time a situation arises where – no matter how vaguely – our fundamental fear or insecurity could be triggered, the mechanism starts to operate. The circumstances of that moment join forces with the momentum of your reactions in similar situations in the past. Like lightning, your mind focuses on the other person and you perform your safety actions.

Look at what happens in a relatively innocuous and superficial situation, for instance, if you're walking down the street and you see someone you know slightly but have no further interest in: you immediately give a little smile of recognition or say 'Hi', and meanwhile you observe how the other responds. Does she expect a more extensive interaction? Notice what happens if you'd already decided to keep walking and the other person stops. Perhaps you also stop immediately, and play the part of being friendly. How long is it before you indicate that you're not interested in continuing the conversation? And do you use an 'in a rush, got to go now' excuse? That's what I usually do, simply out of laziness and fear of hurting the other (i.e. fear of my own guilty conscience about this). But sometimes I try being open and direct, and say pleasantly that I don't want to stop for a long chat and don't want to arrange to meet another time. I realise that this may be hurtful, but I'm also not creating false expectations that would make it necessary to be even more hurtful at a later stage. For me, this is a moment of liberation from my own fearful mind.

The entire mental construction of our self-image is thus unstable by nature, and constantly requires energy to maintain. Yet there's a lot of difference in how successful the mind is at doing this. Some people are very skilled at maintaining a positive self-image, and others much less so. Some have a successful or 'healthy' ego, because they manage to fulfil the conditions that permit them to feel worthwhile. Less successful egos don't manage to do this, so they're more often weighed down by feelings of fear and inferiority. The reason for this lies mainly in the basic rules in the second layer of the identity. If these are unattainable or mutually contradictory, then this is a source of distress and self-rejection. For example, if you've learned that you must never make errors or mistakes, must never get angry and never lose your self-control, then you have a problem, because regardless of how perfectionist the pattern in the third layer of your identity is, it will never manage to obey all those rules. Moreover, perfectionism itself creates a host of problems (such as not having enough time for relaxation or being with your loved ones). Avoiding self-rejection then causes so much stress and rejection from others that on balance the outcome is negative: the harder you work in order to be perfect, the deeper you sink into the pit of negative feelings. This often leads to what we now call 'burnout': you completely burn up in the fire of the battle against your fear of failure.

Another example is so common that we hardly recognise it as an unsuccessful ego. Many people, on average slightly more men than women, have an almost impossible rule in their identity: that it's wrong to have feelings. It takes an incredible amount of energy every day to suppress feelings. The resulting emotional poverty must then be compensated with artificial feelings, also known as 'kicks': excitement and sensation, generated by chemical means if necessary. This suppresses natural feelings even more. And precisely because it's the painful and distressing feelings that are the hardest to suppress, this identity construction usually creates a lot of misery. This phenomenon will be explained in more detail in the next chapter.

Some people learn a very strange and difficult rule: that it's selfish to be happy. One of my clients, I'll call her Angela, had a slightly older brother who had a life-threatening illness for many years during her childhood. The parents lived under constant stress, and gave all their attention to her brother. If Angela was happy, her parents thought she was being very selfish, because her brother might die! In that way, she learned that it's bad to be happy and to request attention for yourself. People who have a basic rule like this in their identity put a tremendous amount of energy into mechanisms to prevent happiness or joy from arising. Someone like this only feels safe in a kind of grey mediocrity. That strategy occasionally fails, of course, and they feel happy for a while, but then self-rejection based on the negative belief follows immediately, in the form of an intense feeling of guilt and self-destructive tendencies. The identity thus contains an inherent inconsistency: you're only allowed to feel good if you're unhappy.

A similar oppressive identity pattern sometimes arises from a strictly religious Christian upbringing, where girls are taught the basic rule that it's bad to be feminine. That's really tough if you're a woman, and is therefore another typical no-win situation. Behaviour patterns will then focus on suppressing expressions of femininity, or conversely – in the phase when you rebel against your upbringing – over-emphasising them, which in both cases results in misery.

In these disruptive mechanisms we see an overarching or 'meta' pattern: the urge to maintain self-control. After all, my whole identity creates the illusion that if I don't keep myself under control, my core of badness (the negative belief!) will emerge and cause damage. This illusion creates its own arguments. Think about it: first there's the negative belief, for instance 'I am weak'. From this follows the basic rule that I must keep myself under control in relation to things that I like, such as drinking alcohol. The behaviour pattern will then put energy into restraining or suppressing the desire for alcoholic drinks. We feel this as a restriction. The frustration about it builds up, to the point where it just turns against the self-control. In a kind of rage, we inwardly say something like 'Well, damned if I care, I'm going to do exactly what I want for a change'. So we go on a binge, and then have a terrible hangover the next day. At that moment, an argument has been created for a new round of self-control, an 'I told you so' argument: 'I told you that you completely mess things up if you don't keep yourself under control'. The negative belief in our own weakness has been confirmed by the failure of the attempt to cover that weakness with self-control.

The same happens with the basic rule that it's wrong to get angry. Someone with this basic rule will have all kinds of anger-suppression mechanisms in their identity, such as always avoiding conflicts or resolving them by amiably giving in. However, the suppressed anger creates a pressure, like when you put your finger over the end of a garden hose. As soon as the pressure is high enough, and something very annoying happens unexpectedly, the self-control fails and the anger erupts so fiercely that it takes the form of an anger attack or aggression. We immediately feel our negative belief of weakness and powerlessness, because in fact our self-control failed. The anger attack is therefore caused by keeping control of anger, and at the same time it creates an 'I told you so' argument for maintaining and increasing that control.

Unattainable and counterproductive rules are thus the main cause of an unsuccessful ego and an above-average level of self-rejection. But in some cases an unsuccessful ego arises if children are systematically not praised enough when they obey the basic rules in the second layer of the identity. Many parents are very quick to reject their children when they don't fulfil the conditions, but are very restrained in giving praise when they do. The underlying fear is that the child will stop doing his best once he's won the praise. For the same reason, it's very rare for parents to randomly praise their child: not because he's just complied with a parenting rule, but purely out of love and respect. This inhibition means that children are actually trained to lack self-confidence; they take on, as it were, their parents' fear that they aren't going to perform well. In consequence, they will be less successful as adults at obtaining the love and approval of others.

This becomes more serious if the child grows up in a situation where her feelings are systematically ignored and her boundaries are violated, as in the case of abuse or mistreatment. A child in this situation learns that her feelings evidently don't matter, so she herself evidently doesn't matter. Even the motivation to attempt to gain other people's love and approval is badly undermined.

Another cause of an unsuccessful self-image is when one or both of the parents use their child to help them with their own problems. For instance, if a depressive mother uses her daughter as a friend and an emotional support, the child might seem very happy about this at first: after all, she's being treated like an adult. But meanwhile she's taking on the responsibility for her mother's happiness. However, the mother doesn't get any happier, she just stays depressed. The daughter therefore learns to believe that her love evidently isn't good enough. And if you believe *that*, you in fact believe that you *yourself* aren't good enough.

If a child grows up in a more or less permanently unsafe environment, for instance if one of the parents suffers from unpredictable anger attacks, as may occur with alcohol addiction, he learns to be constantly on guard. As a result, he develops a fundamental feeling of unsafety, which seriously obstructs his attempts to gain other people's love and approval. That feeling of unsafety is worse if the unsafe situation occurs when the child is very young. Premature babies and babies hospitalised for long periods also have an above-average tendency to develop anxiety disorders in adulthood, so they often find it difficult to maintain a successful ego.

To summarise, an unsuccessful ego thus arises because the person concerned has unattainable or contradictory rules in the second layer of the identity, or has not acquired sufficient self-confidence and feelings of safety to comply with those rules. In fact, there is failure of the layers covering the negative belief, 'holes' often appear in them, so the self-rejection shows through again, time after time. Sometimes this takes the form of an almost constant 'but actually' feeling in relation to everything you do: 'but actually I'm completely worthless'; 'but actually I don't really matter', and so on. Or it can be manifested in dark moods, extreme dependency, addiction, compulsiveness or anxieties. In mainstream psychology, the term 'neurosis' will then often be used, but there's actually only a gradual difference between a healthy ego and a neurotic ego, i.e. the extent to which it succeeds in covering its fundamental negative self-image with other people's love and approval. From a spiritual perspective, the healthy ego is in fact slightly further from home than the neurotic one, because successfully covering your negative belief means that your natural state of being is also buried more deeply under your identity. There will be more about this in the second part of the book. First, however, we will continue with our research on the misunderstandings during the development of our identity, and how they ensure that the way we enter into relationships is also the cause of their failure.

7

Stagnations in the growth of consciousness

In this world
Hate never yet dispelled hate.
Only love dispels hate.
This is the law,
Ancient and inexhaustible.

Buddha

So far we've looked at the development and layered structure of our identity, and seen how that identity is focused on gaining other people's love and approval to cover our negative belief about ourselves. But our identity isn't static: it changes over time due to the need of our consciousness to grow and the influence of circumstances. An adult's identity has the same layered structure as when he was a teenager, but yet it hasn't stayed the same. This is because our consciousness has the tendency to want to expand, to develop towards more knowledge, more insight, more love, more realisation. And if that development is blocked by self-rejection, it will manifest in striving for more approval, more possessions, more pleasure, more status; in short, for growth of some kind or another.

As our consciousness grows we see two alternating phases: identification and transcendence. Let's look first at the development from a baby to adulthood, and distinguish the two phases within this. Initially, a baby has no 'self-consciousness' at all; she is, so to speak, completely merged with her limited experiential world. This might seem a bit like the 'becoming one with the universe' in the highest spiritual state of being, but in fact it's precisely the opposite, because the baby is totally unaware of being merged. She's at the mercy of her own limited experiences of 'pleasant' and 'painful'.

During the first year of life, the baby gradually develops a consciousness of her own body, and also becomes completely identified with it: the child *is* her body. You could say that here the mind loses itself in its own body.

When language development begins, around the age of one to two years, the first sense of an inner world arises, starting with the emotions. The child's consciousness then identifies completely with the newly discovered emotions, and at the same time she gains some awareness of her body. This awareness creates, as it were, a slight distance between the 'I' and the body. The self is no longer only body, but is transcending this stage. The child no longer *is* her body, but rather *has* a body.

When the child is a little older, she develops a sense of the rational processes in the mind, and then starts to identify with the 'thinking I'. As a result, she gains some awareness of her emotions. She no longer completely identifies with those emotions, and is able to transcend them. The child no longer *is* her emotions, but rather *has* emotions.

Thus we see that through the identification with a higher state of consciousness, the lower state becomes the object of that higher consciousness. In other words, what was first the 'self', the subject, then becomes – because it has been transcended – the object of the higher state of consciousness. That higher state then becomes the new 'self', the new subject. Body-consciousness ('I' and 'body' are one) becomes consciousness of the body (I have a body), while the recently discovered emotions assume the role of 'I' ('I' and 'emotions' are one). In the next stage, this emotion-consciousness changes into consciousness of emotions, while the recently discovered rational mind takes over the role of 'I'. And in the stage of growth subsequent to this – we then arrive in the spiritual area – we can, from a higher consciousness, let go of the identification with our own stream of thoughts, and hence no longer *be* our thoughts, but rather *have* thoughts.

The above is a simplified account of more complex stages of growth, but this is the essence: each time the mind opens itself to a higher form of consciousness, it will fully identify with it, and from there it can transcend and include the lower state of consciousness. And I emphasise 'can', because usually some or all of this goes wrong: the growth of consciousness stagnates in two possible ways.

The first form of stagnation occurs if the mind doesn't succeed sufficiently in opening itself to a higher stage of growth. It's usually because of fear or deep feelings of unsafety that the self wants to cling to the current stage of development, and sees new, higher stages as a threat to its existence. Stagnation at the body stage results in a kind of 'body narcissism', in the emotion stage it results in egocentricity, and in the rational stage it results in spiritual standstill: the inability to go beyond the conceptual mind. The first form of stagnation is therefore a kind of becoming 'stuck' in, or completely merging with the current identity, so that change and growth are blocked. For convenience, I call this form 'merging'.

In the second form of stagnation, the mind successfully opens itself to a higher stage of growth, but instead of integrating the recently transcended stage into its consciousness, it rejects it. I call this process 'dissociation'. It is caused by the negative belief, which causes every increase in 'self-consciousness' to immediately change into self-rejection. Dissociation from the body-consciousness results in adults who neglect their physical health, who don't engage in sports or exercise, or who hate their body and feel ugly. Dissociation from the emotion-consciousness results in arrogance and the inability to enter into emotional relationships. Dissociation from the rational consciousness can only occur at a higher stage of consciousness, for instance through extreme practice of certain forms of conceptless meditation, in which the thinking mind completely stops for a time. In short, stagnation by dissociation results in people who try to suppress important parts of their identity, with varying degrees of success. Successful suppression results in a more or less permanent amputation of the suppressed part of consciousness. If the suppression is not entirely successful, then the person remains entangled in constantly rejecting and fighting against this part of their identity.

The two mechanisms of stagnation – merging and dissociation – continue to operate after adulthood. Stagnation by merging is very hard to see in yourself, because the total identification with a certain state of consciousness excludes all reflection about it. It's easier to see it in other people, for instance in some young parents who identify so completely with their new role as parents that they're not at all open to any critical reflection of that role. Sometimes they lose most of their childless friends, who can't stand to only talk about children and parenting. Given the very limited capacity for reflection, anyone who's in a 'merging phase' of this kind usually has no self-doubt, at least in relation to the merged part of the self-image. However, this shouldn't be mistaken for self-confidence, because the absence of doubt is merely a compulsive protection from the deep fear of self-rejection. In difficult times, people in the merging phase are inclined to feel that they're victims of their circumstances, and feel dependent on other people. A more subtle form of merging can sometimes be seen after an intensive training session or workshop in which participants have conquered certain fears and broken through certain blocks. They then often fall into the trap of identifying with their new euphoric state of consciousness, and really believe that they've solved their problems once and for all. If they find that this isn't true, they become terribly disappointed and the 'stagnation by merging' often switches immediately to 'stagnation by dissociation', i.e. dissociation from their desire for growth.

You can recognise dissociation in yourself as follows: each time you've discovered an obstructive pattern or automatic response in yourself, there's a strong tendency to want to get rid of it. We profoundly believe that development means we must fight and eliminate our 'lower' automatic mental responses – such as inhibitions, dependencies, addictions, and compulsions – in order to become a better and happier person. This is one of the main misunderstandings that sustain our ego, and therefore our suffering. I will give an example from my own rich experience of stagnations by dissociation.

I mentioned earlier that I'm the youngest and an 'afterthought' in a family of six children, and one of the negative beliefs that I acquired was 'I am weak'. In addition to the basic rule 'you must be nice', which resulted in my 'nice guy' image, I also learned the basic rule 'you must be smarter'. I developed a strong ambition to be smarter than the rest, to cover my feelings of inferiority. Cleverness became part of my image: always making witty remarks and drawing people's attention to mistakes in their reasoning. The pattern that's responsible for this is called arrogance. People whose opinions differed from my own (especially those who were politically right-wing or religious) were pleasantly yet mercilessly torn to shreds, either in speech or in writing. When I started therapy and training after my serious burnout, I gradually became aware of this pattern. By reflecting from a higher state of consciousness, i.e. the rational mind, I was able to see my total identification with this superiority pattern. Something else that is clearly evident in this example, incidentally, is that my use of logic and reasoning seemed to be rational (and hence superior), but in reality that was not the case. After all, the motivation behind it was merely an attempt to protect myself from my feelings of inferiority.

Anyway, as soon as I became aware of my own arrogance, my immediate reaction was condemnation, and I tried to get rid of it. Influenced by my study of Buddhism, I actually tried to acquire a new image: the tolerant and compassionate sage. My arrogance was suppressed, and for a long time I thought it had gone. But then it would suddenly come back at unexpected moments, and to my shame I noticed that I sometimes looked down on other people as religious idiots or nasty right-wingers. Later I realised that my attempt to free myself of my arrogance was only working at the external level. I certainly behaved less arrogantly, even developed a kind of reticence, and became almost timid, so that people wouldn't regard me as arrogant. Meanwhile, the arrogance lived on below the surface, and when it sometimes re-emerged, the consequence was annoyance and self-rejection.

Maybe you've also experienced something like this yourself, for instance after doing some therapy or training. You really tried your best to eliminate certain harmful or destructive patterns from your past, and to a certain extent you succeeded. But from time to time you find that at a deeper level nothing's changed at all, and the old trait that you thought had gone rears its head again, cool as can be. You're then very disappointed in yourself: 'I thought I'd left all that behind me long ago'; and filled with self-rejection: 'how stupid, weak or bad of me, that I still have that'.

Most forms of therapy and training don't help much beyond dissociating from a self-rejecting pattern, without understanding that in fact a 'meta' self-rejection (a rejection of the self-rejection) is taking place here. And in practical terms, dissociation brings about some improvement in your situation: the negative pattern caused much more damage when you were less aware of it, and to some extent it's been deactivated by the dissociation. But at the same time it starts to act as a kind of ballast, like a dead weight that you constantly carry around. It's true that your newly acquired image is nicer for yourself and others, but it also slows down further development.

So why would a dissociated pattern be a hindrance for further growth? Surely it seems only logical that you need to eliminate negative patterns like arrogance, jealousy, dependence, and addiction before you can grow further? The mistake in saying this is that we're not seeing that the negative pattern is actually a blocked or distorted version of a positive natural quality. In Chapter 5 we saw that the qualities of our natural state that are rejected in our youth come back in a twisted form in the ego. For instance, altruism after rejection becomes helpaholism, honesty changes into abruptness, integrity into rigidity, strength into toughness, and intelligence into arrogance.

In the example of my own arrogance, its suppression caused a block of my natural intelligence. In the classroom I didn't dare ask questions for fear of looking stupid. So I still clung to the image of 'smarter than the rest'. And if the teacher asked an open question and no one else knew the answer, I kept my mouth shut, because otherwise everyone would see how proud of myself I was to be the smartest. In this way, suppressing my arrogance also created a block of my intellectual and spiritual development. In the second half of this book, you'll find out how that tendency towards dissociation can change to integration.

In the same way, you can see that people who, for instance, try to suppress their toughness also inhibit their strength. Or if you suppress your compulsive inclination to help people, your altruism is also blocked. In my book *Beyond Addiction* I wrote that fighting an addiction not only maintains that addiction but also blocks the development of spiritual aspirations that lie behind it. In *The End of Upbringing* I described how parents who try to combat negative traits in their children actually – by doing this – reinforce them, and obstruct the underlying natural feelings of self-esteem that they wish to encourage.

Now take a good look at the so-called negative traits from which you're trying to free yourself. And then look first at how unsuccessful you are in doing this. Also, look at the price you pay for this attempt at dissociation and amputation. Are you fighting your weakness and laziness? Then see how your natural need for self-expression becomes even more blocked. Are you trying to get rid of your need for superficial sex? Then see how your natural capacity to love becomes more restricted. Do you hate feeling so dismal? Then see how you become increasingly alienated from your natural source of joy. Every attempt to kill a part of your self-image, however oppressive that part might feel, adds to the oppression, and takes you further away from your natural state of being. Thus even the spiritual quest for enlightenment and egolessness can be completely blocked by your attempts to kill the ego. In the words of a great Dutch poet:

... what is dead is dead,
but what is killed lives on uncurbed,
lives on thereafter less disturbed
than what's alive, not having died.

Martinus Nijhoff (1894-1953)
from: *Het uur U* (H-Hour)

So can you see how that one fundamental mistake – not recognising our perfect nature – launches a whole series of subsequent mistakes? First there's the mother of all misunderstandings, our negative belief that we're inadequate and therefore not good as we are, but that we can become good by fulfilling all kinds of conditions. Then we make our self-esteem dependent on other people's love and approval. We develop a wide range of automatic responses with which we try to gain that love and approval, and try to avoid rejection. And this entire complicated and uncertain game of tricks and manipulations is covered by an image of perfection, by an 'everything is hunky-dory with me' show.

In striving for more happiness, two kinds of stagnation constantly arise: merging and dissociation. The fear of rejection results each time in merging with safe parts of the self-image, while self-rejection results in dissociation from unsafe parts of the self-image. We become stuck in our identification with patterns and roles that provide us with other people's love or approval, and we try to get rid of aspects of our self-image that we ourselves find unacceptable and could therefore be rejected by other people. Instead of playing the role of mother or father, for instance, we merge with this role, we *are* a mother or father. We don't *have* a job as a scientist or baker, we *are* a scientist or baker. In general, we don't *have* thoughts and emotions, we *are* those thoughts and emotions.

And if, eventually, our consciousness does actually open up to a higher and wider perspective of ourselves, then the other polarity of the fundamental misunderstanding comes into action: we look with disgust at that past merging and try to get rid of it as soon as possible, and identify with a new role that's more appropriate for the new consciousness. From the one merging we move via the subsequent dissociation to a new merging, always clinging to a self-image that must hide the belief in our own inadequacy and must provide us with other people's approval. Look around you and see this dance of misunderstandings. When people are stuck in the merging phase, you can see them becoming more passive or more anxious, or depressed. When people are stuck in the dissociation phase, you mainly see escapist behaviour into sex, drugs and rock and roll, with addiction as the relatively final destination. Merging and dissociation are the two legs that constantly take us along the road to other people's love and approval, alienated from our own nature. Fear of rejection and self-rejection are the two big sticks that keep us on this road. Anxiety neuroses and depression are the result of merging, guilt feelings, and addictions the result of dissociation.

Analyse the extent to which you're stuck in a merging or a dissociation, bearing in mind that it's actually possible to be stuck in both at the same time, but then in relation to different patterns. For example, you can be merged with your role as a mother and at the same time dissociated from your urge to rebel. One way to analyse yourself is to look at situations where someone particularly annoys you. If you find it difficult to give a name to that annoyance, if you don't really understand why that person annoys you so much, then there's a chance that you yourself are merged with the same pattern as that person. If, on the other hand, you can see very clearly what the other person does wrong, for instance wanting to be the centre of attention in a group, then there's a good chance that you yourself are dissociated from the inclination to seek attention. In general, when someone's behaviour annoys you, it's either because you're unconsciously the same yourself (merging), or because you very consciously don't want to be like that (dissociation).

During my training to become a trainer, I was taught by someone whose behaviour often infuriated me: he could confront people in a dreadfully dominant and unfriendly way, constantly setting himself up in a superior position. I later realised that he was using, with no inhibition whatsoever, the very qualities that I – as a 'nice guy' – had been suppressing in myself all my life. 'But,' you might object, 'was what you saw in him not true then?' Well yes, perhaps it was, but the fact that it annoyed me so much was really a consequence of my own dissociation. Now that I've stopped dissociating from my 'nice guy' pattern, and have learned to integrate it in my self-image, I'm no longer so bothered by such dominant attention-seekers. 'But,' you might also object, 'haven't you now become a dominant attention seeker yourself, instead of a nice guy?' Well no, that's the great thing about converting your dissociation into integration (more on this in Part 2): by integrating the self-rejecting pattern, it changes back into the original and natural quality of which it was a distorted version. The 'nice guy' syndrome, once the self-rejection and fear of rejection have been discarded, becomes again what in essence it always was: pure kindness!

If your self-analysis reveals that you are indeed merged with certain patterns and/or dissociated from other patterns, don't be disappointed or angry with yourself, but congratulate yourself! Recognising your stagnations is the first and most important step towards learning to integrate them. Later in this book you'll see that there's no need to fight against those self-rejecting patterns in order to become free of them. On the contrary, fighting against them creates – in the best-case scenario – a slightly less negative way to obtain other people's love and approval; but even then you're still a long way from home, from the house of your natural state. Mostly, however, it only creates more self-rejection, behind an increasingly restrictive image of poise, success, spirituality, or whatever it is you're aiming for. So start by recognising your self-rejecting patterns with kindness: it's not your fault that you've got them, it's not anyone's fault; and moreover, everyone has them, you're no different than anyone else in this. Your self-rejecting patterns are the building blocks with which your illusory self-image has been built on the foundation of your negative belief. To recognise and accept them is a reason for celebration: you're on your way back to the house of your natural state, where you haven't dared to go until now – for fear of that snake, for fear of your belief that you're basically not good enough.

8

The creation of suffering

Rest in natural great peace
This exhausted mind
Beaten helpless by karma and neurotic thought,
Like the relentless fury of the pounding waves
In the infinite ocean of samsara.

Nyoshul Kenpo, Tibetan Buddhist master
(1932-1999)

We have seen up to now that self-rejection is the core of our entire self-image, the engine that drives our constant need for other people's love and approval, and the main reason for our repeated attempts to kill certain parts of our self-image, once we become aware of them. However, the mechanism of merging and dissociation is not only involved in patterns of thinking, feeling, and behaviour, but also at a more subtle level, namely in all individual painful emotions. Self-rejection is basically the cause of all forms of mental and emotional suffering! Self-rejection is the core of our ego, and hence the engine of the vicious process of misery that Buddhists call 'samsara'. So how does this mechanism work? The following explanation of the cause of suffering is very important to free yourself from that vicious process. But the explanation is not intended as a faith or philosophy that you have to accept on other people's authority. You must check the validity of this theory *yourself*, by learning to look at your mind in the manner described later in this book. And it's only then that this spiritual knowledge will really start to 'work'.

What exactly happens when you suffer from a distressing emotion? First there's a cause that evokes the distress, known as the 'trigger'. This can be a situation or a person, or the thought of a situation or person, with a direct or indirect reference to a painful situation in the past. Immediately after the trigger, the distressing emotion arises in you: fear, anger, jealousy, or whatever. For the first few seconds or minutes there's a complete merging with that emotion, you're completely one with it, you *are* that emotion. In some people this merging lasts much longer; they – so to speak – get stuck in it and act purely on the basis of that emotion. But many people, especially those who have developed some self-reflection through training or therapy, will after a short time become aware of the distress. They no longer *are* that emotion, they *have* that emotion. This in itself is a very important step towards more spiritual development; the only problem is that this progress is immediately negated by dissociation: we resist the negative emotion, we don't want to feel it, and the mind starts to swirl with thoughts and counter-thoughts. Unfortunately, this resistance only strengthens the negative emotion, which also makes the thoughts more intense, and these in turn increase the distress. In short, here again you recognise the vicious circle of the rejection, which only exacerbates what's being rejected.

If you compare your mind to a box of grasshoppers, and your painful emotion is one of those grasshoppers, constantly jumping around in your mind, then our usual reaction to that painful grasshopper can be compared to kicking the whole box. The result is even more painful grasshoppers in your head. In general terms, that's how we deal with our painful emotions. I will now give a more precise description of how negative emotions work.

1 *The trigger*
First there is a situation or thought that has an apparent similarity to a particular pain from the past. This can be a conscious painful expe-

rience from the past, or an unconscious distressing memory, for instance from your early childhood, when your natural spontaneity was rejected and you had to learn to fulfil conditions.

2 The identification

Identification immediately arises: there is an 'I' feeling that appropriates the memory, in other words, there is a phase of merging with the memory of suffering. How does this identification with the apparent suffering take place? Through self-rejection. Something that is initially a memory of suffering, and therefore merely a semblance of suffering, is made real by the additional experience of an 'I' that is evidently not good enough, or stupid, bad or weak, or whatever your negative belief might be.

3 The reaction

As soon as the memory of pain changes into a real experience of pain, the reaction follows. We immediately do everything we can to get rid of that pain, in order to again fulfil the conditions that allow us to feel good as soon as possible. Those attempts can either be directed against the person or situation that triggered the painful memory, or against yourself: it just depends on the patterns you've developed for this. Note carefully: up to this point, the whole process is still automatic, we're not aware of it. It's all part of the merging phase.

4 The reflection and the dissociation

Sooner or later, depending on the degree of self-reflection that we've developed, we become aware that we have the distressing emotion. At the same time, the unconscious self-rejection also shifts to the conscious level. We're now aware of the distress, we think we're very wrong to have this distress, and try to get rid of it as soon as possible! This is the start of the attempt to dissociate, and the open fight against the distressing emotion. And the bizarre thing now is that it only increases the distress!

The initially unconscious vicious circle of apparent suffering and identification with it through self-rejection (merging) thus continues – via self-reflection at a conscious or 'meta' level – as dissociation. You probably recognise it: at an earlier stage you only reacted to the cause of your misery without being aware of it. But as soon as reflection and 'self-consciousness' are added, you suddenly become conscious of the self-rejection: you start to think you're stupid for feeling stupid. You think you're pathetic for not being assertive. You get angry with yourself because you can't control your anger. You hate yourself because you don't love yourself. In short, you reject yourself for having self-rejecting feelings! It's distress squared.

'Yes, but', you might object, 'surely that's necessary! Am I supposed to just accept my self-rejection and learn to live with it?' No, not at all, that wouldn't even be possible: once something has become conscious it can't be made unconscious again. As soon as you've become aware of a self-rejecting emotion, the merging phase has gone and you can't go back to it. Growth of consciousness is a one-way street, and it's wonderful that it is! The only thing we then need to learn is not to fall into the trap of dissociation, and instead to take the route of integration. This is what the second half of this book is about.

But first you must really understand, in its entirety, the complex pattern with which we create our own suffering. Because there's yet another complicating factor, another mistake on top of the previous ones: after the first mistake of self-rejection, then the second mistake of constructing a self-image to cover that self-rejection and obtain other people's approval, and then the third mistake of switching to dissociation each time we become aware of a pattern or a negative emotion, there follows a fourth mistake, which conceals all the others: the projection of our emotions onto other people and onto our circumstances.

In literature, a kind of reverse projection is sometimes used as a means to evoke certain emotions in the reader, by attributing those emotions to material objects:

It lay there, listless and weary: the Hotel du Nord, once the pride of the provincial town, now confined between a bank and a supermarket, sus-

pecting nothing of the spectacular romance that would take place there that same summer.

Everyone knows that a hotel can't feel listless and weary, or ever suspect what's going to happen, but the reverse projection evokes these emotions in the reader. And the same in these blues lyrics:

*My baby, she ain't coming back no more,
and now I'm sitting in my lonely room...*

The man sings that his room is lonely, but in reality, of course, that's what he is himself. We all know that rooms can't be lonely. Yet it's easy to look back in your own memory and recall that when your mood is gloomy, the cheerful spring weather is suddenly not so cheerful anymore, the interior decoration of your home is just completely dreadful, and your lovely friend isn't really that great after all. While conversely, when you're in a euphoric state of mind, even the most appalling autumn weather has its charm, and the most irritating colleague is actually quite OK.

However, the projection mechanism goes far beyond merely projecting our moods onto our surroundings. For every painful feeling, we project the cause – and hence the responsibility for it – onto the person or situation that triggered the pain. Look at how it works. Your colleague says, 'You're always the last one to step up whenever some extra work needs to be done'. This remark makes you feel unappreciated, so your colleague is an annoying, arrogant, conceited pain in the butt. Or your partner confesses that she's been having an affair for a while. You feel terribly hurt, betrayed and abandoned, so then your partner is terribly wrong, selfish, mean, or untrustworthy. But is that really true? Or is the projection mechanism in operation here? Let's now make a precise analysis of this occurrence, on the basis of the four stages on pages 62 and 63:

1. Your colleague says something, your partner confesses to something. This triggers a memory of distress and suffering, based on previous rejection and self-rejection.

2. Immediately there's an 'I' feeling that identifies itself with this memory by rejecting itself. The memory of a feeling becomes 'I *am* that feeling'. We merge with it.
3. This 'I' doesn't want to feel like that; resistance arises, and we engage in a fight with the feeling.
4. Upon reflection, a meta-rejection can also arise: you hate yourself because you reject yourself, and you try to dissociate from this painful feeling. But whether this reflection takes place is irrelevant for the next step.
5. The fight against the painful feeling is directed against whomever or whatever triggered the feeling: the colleague or the partner causes the suffering here, and must therefore stop doing this. The colleague must apologise, the partner must end her affair; in short, the trigger must stop.

Do you see what's irrational about this? It's the old story of shooting the messenger who brings bad news. It's like blaming the doctor who's found that you have cancer. In reality, the person or situation that triggered the painful feeling isn't the cause of it at all. The cause lies in your own fundamental misunderstanding that you're not as good as you are. And to keep this painful feeling covered, you've learned to outsource your self-esteem to other people. *That* is why they can so easily cause this edifice of borrowed self-esteem to collapse. Each time this happens, you actually receive a painfully clear message: 'Your strategy doesn't work, your self-esteem is phoney!' But because you're completely unaware of your striving for other people's approval, you also don't recognise the projection of your self-rejection onto the person who made you feel it. By projecting your negative feelings onto other people and circumstances, you condemn yourself to powerlessness, you lose the capacity to resolve those negative feelings yourself, and you surrender yourself to the caprice of others.

Projection is the ultimate concealer of reality, the most effective veiling mechanism of samsara, the vicious circle of suffering and our resistance to it. It's the engine that drives the endless complaints of people: my mother should respect me, my partner shouldn't leave me, my child shouldn't be unhappy, my car shouldn't break down, my colleague shouldn't misunderstand me. My house should be bigger, my car newer, my work more interesting, my body more beautiful; I should be healthy, people should be more aware, there shouldn't be war, the world shouldn't go wrong. Our most individual complaints have been recycled countless times already. Over and over again, they're the same projections of the same self-rejection. 'Yes, but', you might wish to object, 'surely people sometimes really hurt each other, and that isn't projection, is it? Surely some things are really wrong, aren't they? And then isn't it logical that you feel unhappy?' Well yes, it is logical that you then feel unhappy, from the standpoint of the veiled state of being in which we usually live. But pay close attention, because this is very subtle: I'm not saying that you shouldn't feel unhappy; after all, that would also be a form of dissociation. I'm only saying that someone who's truly free of self-rejection and fear of rejection, someone who's in contact with his natural state, which is full of love and approval, someone like that never feels powerless or a victim of other people's behaviour. Take a good look at your reproaches of others, or your rejection of people or situations; are they really bad or wrong because they evoked pain in you? Turn it around and look at times in your past when others felt hurt by your behaviour. Was it really your intention to hurt that other person? Be honest, how long is it since you deliberately and gladly caused pain or grief to someone else? It's even possible that you've never actually done that! If you've ever caused someone pain, then it was out of powerlessness or anger, out of fear or stupidity, out of ignorance or even with good intentions. Other people are just like you! They too are dependent on your approval, and if you sometimes fail to give it, they're hurt and angry with you. Can you see how we've got one another trapped with our neediness for love and approval on the one hand, and the projection of our self-rejection on the other?

You can analyse this in yourself every day: each time you feel reproach towards someone, or resistance to a situation, in reality a painful feeling of self-rejection is evoked, plus your automatic resistance to that feeling, as well as your projection of it onto the other person or situation, which makes you feel powerless and the victim of your circumstances. Sometimes you have to search really carefully, because our mind is accustomed to taking its own projections very seriously: 'What Pete said to me was really horrible', or 'It's just so awful that I had to get a flat tyre, right at this moment'. But if you practise (there's more about this later), you'll see with increasing clarity that behind those reproaches lies a feeling of having failed. That you think you're stupid if Pete makes a rejecting remark against you. That you think you're lazy because you should have changed that tyre a long time ago. In short, if you look closely you'll learn to see your self-rejection in every painful or distressing situation.

So do we have to learn to stop projecting? That's an understandable reaction, and fits with the above-described tendency to dissociate: if it's not good, we must get rid of it. But no, dissociation of projection doesn't work, because after all, projection itself is a consequence of dissociation. Trying to get rid of projections would be fairly disastrous, just like thinking that you must stop thinking; it would pretty much drive you crazy. But you *can* become aware of the projection mechanism, and integrate it in the image of yourself and reality. Someone who's done groundbreaking work in helping us to see and free ourselves from our projections is Byron Katie (see Appendix 1). The second part of this book deals with how you can become free of the restrictive double act of dissociation and projection. Because isn't it rather restrictive to always be dependent on other people's love and approval? To be hurt every time others don't give us that approval? To always depend on other people and circumstances for our happiness and self-esteem? That isn't how we really are! That's the result of a series of mistakes, which all start with and are nurtured by our fundamental misunderstanding of our perfect nature. All those mistakes are manifested in the relationship that we have with ourselves, and in the projection of that: our relationship with others. And the ultimate crowning glory of this series of mistakes is – maybe you've already guessed – the love relationship! Read on, and shudder at how the most beautiful thing that exists is also the absolute zenith of our suffering.

9

The free market of love and approval

*You could search the whole world
and not find anyone more worthy
of your love than yourself.*

Buddha

In the last chapter I explained that projecting our self-rejection onto others is the last in a long succession of mistakes. But in fact there's yet another one after that: having projected our emotions onto another person, we then proceed to enter into a relationship with them! And that puts the lid on it! That is the final and definitive step by which we give up our own responsibility for our happiness. With this, all earlier mental and emotional mistakes are solidified into a rigid system of dependencies. If our entire identity is aimed at seeking other people's love and approval, relationships are a kind of reciprocal agreement to create stability in that mutual dependency. In exactly the same way that an employment contract is intended to provide some security in the relationship with your employer, we enter into relationships at different levels with colleagues, acquaintances, friends, and lovers to create stability in the supply of our daily dose of love and approval. We're relatively selective in this: we need more approval from some people, and less or none at all from others. Have you ever wondered why you like some people and don't like others? Just because some people happen to be nicer than others, we usually think. But isn't it a bit strange that other people like people that you don't like? And that some people think you're nice and others don't? Take a moment to reflect on this most self-evident phenomenon, and see that something's not quite right. After all, if 'nice' and 'not nice' were qualities of the people themselves, then there would be 'nice' and 'not nice' people in an absolute sense, and everyone would only like the 'nice' people, and no one would like the 'not nice' people. But in reality, even the person who – in your opinion – is the nastiest piece of work imaginable is liked by some people, and your very best friend might be seen as horrible by someone else. Of course there are also objective differences between people in terms of how friendly and approachable they are. But our evaluation of others is largely based on a projection of our own emotions. How does that work?

Every person's identity is a unique construction of methods and automatic responses to conceal his negative belief and ensure he gets other people's love and approval. The use of those methods is mostly subconscious, it's just what we consider normal in our interactions with others. And in fact there's nothing wrong with this; it only creates a lot of misery if you're not aware of it. So this isn't an argument to stop caring about what anyone thinks about you, or to stop giving others any love and approval. After all, that would itself be another instance of dissociation. No, just try to observe the methods and tricks that you use, without judging them.

Here are a few examples of the various and sometimes opposite ways in which we try to obtain love, affection or approval. The nice guy does it by always being kind, by giving in to other people and putting them at ease. But there are also people who do the opposite and try to gain respect by scoring points off other people and always knowing best. The show-off parades his talents to win praise. But there are also people who try to win praise with their modest and reticent manner or by admiring others. There are people who share their emotions with others, and bond with them in this way. And there are people who keep their emotions to themselves, and gain approval through a cool demeanour of steady reliability.

This is just a small selection as there are so many other possibilities. Moreover, each person doesn't always use the same strategy, but sometimes switches between several options to win people. I myself, for instance, often use the nice guy method, but sometimes also the 'I am smarter than the rest' manner, occasionally seasoned with a dash of 'anti-authoritarian hippy', or a pinch of 'romantic eccentric', and in recent years a generous splash of the 'helping professional'. And I'm attracted to people who, for instance, have a modest manner, are slightly vulnerable or shy, and have the courage to talk about their emotions and problems. On the other hand, I have an aversion to attention-seekers and braggers, dominant people and people who behave unreasonably and show no consideration to me.

Thus, we like some people because we can relate to one or more of their qualities, and dislike others because we're annoyed by one or more of their qualities. But we've already seen that projection is the real reason why someone annoys you! You're then either still merged with that annoying quality yourself, or conversely you try to dissociate from it. You dislike someone because she displays annoying qualities that you also have yourself without knowing it (merging), or that you absolutely don't want to have (any more) yourself (dissociation). And you like someone because she has pleasant qualities that you also have yourself, or would like to have. Can you see how wonderfully this works? Because we're alienated from our natural self-esteem, our mind is focused on obtaining other people's esteem; and the qualities we esteem in the other in exchange for this are our own projected pleasant qualities! We run away from our self-rejection, and the qualities we reject in the other are our own projected unpleasant qualities.

As a result of those many possible combinations, within everyone's identity there's a highly varied market of supply and demand of love and approval. There are people who can get along with almost everyone, others who are very selective in their contacts, and yet others who are so ensnared in their self-rejection that it's almost impossible for them to still like anyone. The stronger your self-condemnation, the stronger your projection of it, and therefore the harsher your judgement of other people. If you're not aware of that self-condemnation and its projection, then you think the other person is stupid, weak, or bad, and you continue to merge with those self-rejecting patterns. However, if it's clear to you that condemning other people is actually self-rejection, then you immediately feel the urge to dissociate from it: you forbid yourself to condemn others, and condemn yourself if nevertheless you do. But unfortunately this only increases your self-rejection.

So is every judgement actually a projection, you might wonder? This is a question with many philosophical consequences that are beyond the scope of this book. From a practical point of view, it's enough to see that in any case every condemnation or rejection is a projection. For example, if you view the behaviour of a drug-addicted car thief as negative, then that in itself isn't a condemnation; you're just making a distinction between socially acceptable behaviour and anti-social or even criminal behaviour. But if you despise and reject that addict as an inferior kind of being after he's broken into your car, then you're projecting a self-rejection onto him. Which self-rejection? It's hard to say. Perhaps it's the confrontation with your fear that you actually can't afford to have a car, and now on top of that there's this damage too. Or it's your feeling of powerlessness that you can't handle. Or you've identified with your car as an extension of your status so much that every scratch on it is a scratch on your soul. Who knows what the car thief will unleash in you? But if you learn to look at it in this way, you can even learn something from a car thief! In general: if you feel seriously aggrieved by another person, unfairly judged, abandoned, abused, neglected, misunderstood, manipulated or hurt, then you can bet your life that your self-rejection has projected itself – with great self-justification – onto the other person. Maybe there really is manipulation, misunderstanding, or injustice as well; that's certainly possible. But as soon as you feel that you're the powerless victim of it, it's your own misunderstanding, injustice, or self-manipulation that's weighing you down.

Another interesting phenomenon on the market of love and approval is the principle of exchange. If the baker says, 'You look stunning today!' then that's quite nice, but if you hear the same thing from the person you've secretly been in love with for months, you're on cloud nine for the rest of the day! If your neighbour says, 'Hey, that's great guitar-playing!' then you're fairly pleased, but if Eric Clapton or Joe Bonamassa (or whoever your guitar idol might be) says the same thing, you'd be totally ecstatic! It's obvious that approval and appreciation have higher value if they come from someone who also receives your approval and appreciation, and have no value whatsoever – or are even irritating – if they come from someone you don't appreciate at all. 'You look stunning today!' spoken by that tiresome, boozy-breathed security guy at work will probably add little to your self-esteem, and will perhaps even be more likely to leave a rather unpleasant feeling. Yet in all those cases you look equally stunning, in the eyes of the baker, or the drunk security guy, or your secret love. The extent to which their approval contributes to your self-esteem is proportionate to how much you appreciate them.

We thus invest our appreciation in others in exchange for their appreciation of us, and with the intention of being appreciated by them. And others do the same with us, because the process is reciprocal. More than that, what you appreciate most in someone is their appreciation of you. Imagine this situation: there's someone in your neighbourhood that you know and quite often encounter, and you don't really like her very much, because of the way she looks, or because of her behaviour, which comes across as standoffish and rejecting; or because she's perhaps a bit arrogant or attention-seeking. You hear stories about her that further confirm your negative opinion; in short, for you, she's someone to avoid. But one day that same person comes up to you and says, 'I'd just like to tell you that I really appreciated what you said at the neighbourhood meeting this week. I thought it was very brave of you, and it's set me thinking. Thank you very much.' Then she says a friendly goodbye and walks on. Do you see what happens now? Your entire projection, which until then you regarded as reality, falls apart in an instant! You were appreciated! And now you'll most likely also start to appreciate her; you'll see her very differently, perhaps you'll even become friends, all depending on the positive qualities that you can project onto each other.

So we're all lifelong speculators on the 'exchange market' of love and approval. And there's another peculiar feature of this market: love and approval can't be passed on like other means of exchange or payment. Think about it: Pete loves his wife Marie, but she loves their gay neighbour Bert, who in turn is madly in love with Pete. In all other economies this would be an excellent deal, with everyone satisfied, but not on the market of love and approval. We only appreciate people who appreciate us and display some qualities that we regard as pleasant. We reject everyone who rejects us and displays qualities that we regard as unpleasant. Imperceptibly but very precisely we keep tally to make sure the appreciation balance doesn't get too far out of equilibrium. Someone who never does anything nice in return will eventually lose our appreciation. And also if someone appreciates us much more than we can return, the deal won't last long. Being over-appreciated can actually feel quite embarrassing (especially for someone who has low self-esteem).

We enter into superficial and variable deals with the baker and the checkout operator: 'Here's your receipt, and have a nice day'. In the case of colleagues, neighbours, and acquaintances, more approval or affection is involved in the exchange. And we invest even more and with greater tenacity in friendships. But the biggest investment of them all, the one with most chance of a high yield and heavy loss, is the love relationship! Past performance does not guarantee future results! In the next chapter you'll read about how we can reach the highest pinnacle of happiness, or the deepest hell of loneliness and abandonment, and via those peaks and troughs often end up in a lowland of dreary co-existence, or a more or less bearable solitary existence.

10

The love relationship

Of course love is eternal.
It's only the partners that change.

Martine Carol, French film actress
(1920-1967)

There are different kinds of love relationships, actually as many kinds as there are combinations of people, but you can broadly distinguish between two kinds in terms of how they arise. One is where the love relationship arises out of another form of relationship: the partners were first colleagues, neighbours, good friends, or just sexual partners for a while, and the love relationship developed later. The other starts with 'falling in love', and a relationship grows out of that. In the first kind, the partners can also be 'in love', but this is not the deepest basis of the relationship: this is more a romantic sentiment depending on the right circumstances. In the second kind, the deepest basis of the relationship is indeed being 'in love', but these feelings can largely or entirely disappear after a while, or re-emerge very occasionally as a romantic sentiment.

The relationship problems that will be explained in this book are found in their purest form in the relationship based on 'falling in love', and in fact are present from the very beginning. In the first kind of relationship there is initially the possibility of the two partners being more independent. In time, however, a number of fundamental misunderstandings will create more or less the same restrictions as in the second kind. I will therefore not discuss the two kinds of relationships separately, and will limit myself to the purest manifestation, the relationship that arose out of 'falling in love'.

'Falling in love' is actually a most remarkable phenomenon. Suddenly there's that one person who seems to be almost a shining light among the grey majority of ordinary human beings. He or she simply radiates a force of attraction. She is charming, sweet, lovely, sexy, beautiful, intelligent, affectionate, warm, and pure. She is decisive or – conversely – endearingly hesitant, very open or intriguingly secretive, pleasantly relaxed about sex or very clear about stating her boundaries. I'm already indicating here how some qualities of the loved one are immediately angled towards a positive interpretation. And this is done by both sides: he is cool or – conversely – endearingly insecure, he is experienced and decisive in the area of sex or very vulnerable and pure, he is wonderfully self-confident and organises everything or he can stand aside and give you lots of space.

You see, the projection game is strong right from the start. There's absolutely no room for more or less objective reflection on whether this man or woman is really a suitable person with whom to have further contact. Once Cupid's golden arrow has struck, everything about the other is interpreted in accordance with the adoration. Even if you're still actually capable of perceiving that someone has certain drawbacks, they're instantly so insignificant compared with that person's tremendously fantastic qualities that they're ignored. There's even an expression for this: we 'see them through the eyes of love'. Another – somewhat more unkind – expression is 'love is blind'.

In the initial phase, when you've just fallen in love and it's still uncertain whether the feeling is mutual, the focus of the mind becomes extremely narrow. The loved one is almost permanently in your thoughts, which work overtime on the question that goes round and round in your head: is your love reciprocated? And how can you find out? There's an incredible intensification of hope and fear, with highly emotive fantasies of being together and eternal happiness, and deep fears of rejection, loneliness and being eternally deprived of this most profound love. And then, in the midst of this tempest of contradictory emotions of hope and fear, you discover that in fact it is mutual. What unimaginable bliss! It is almost impossible to believe that this most beautiful, most adorable, most fascinating, most talented, most exciting and most special of all beings thinks that I am the most beautiful, most adorable, most fascinating, most talented, most exciting and most special of all beings! It's sometimes literally beyond comprehension, and we experience the highest attainable happiness on the market of love and approval: '... *to love and be loved in return.*'*

Perhaps your reaction to the above description was rather sceptical, or you thought it was all a bit exaggerated or even slightly mocking. Then it's likely that you're not in love at the moment. It's very striking that when you're not in love you almost can't imagine that you ever could be so in love, even if you have been in the past. What especially seems quite strange – or even really stupid – is the absolute and total lack of any relative perspective whatsoever, the superlative degree of ultimate admiration. 'That will never happen to me again, I'm far too grown-up for that now', is what many people think. Others look back on their earlier 'infatuations' as a beautiful dream: nice while it lasted, but not particularly relevant. And yet others spend their whole life going round lamenting the absence of their lost love.

Be that as it may, being 'in love' is still something highly remarkable, and the way we think about it is usually very different from the way we think *while* we're in love. Now that we've seen in the previous chapters how our entire identity is aimed at getting other people's love and approval to cover our deepest self-rejection, and how for this purpose we merge with safe qualities and dissociate from unsafe qualities, and how we then project these qualities onto other people, in short, now that this is somewhat figured out, we can investigate what really happens to us when we 'fall in love'.

---

* From: 'Nature Boy', written by eden ahbez and sung by Nat King Cole.

In addition to the usual mechanisms with which we try to maintain a positive self-image, when we fall in love something extra happens, something unique: what we put on the market of love and approval is nothing less than the deepest basis of those covering mechanisms, our deepest self-rejection. Because when you're in love you get the impression that the other person can 'undo' this deepest self-rejection. After all, this self-rejection developed during your childhood, influenced by your parents' rejection of you. For this reason, you always fall in love with someone who has the same rejecting qualities as (one of) your parents, yet who also gives you a clear impression that he won't reject you, but – on the contrary – will love you unconditionally. It's that combination of old rejection and new, apparently unconditional love that makes someone irresistibly attractive. Everything that went wrong in the past will now be put right; everything that was rejected will now be accepted and embraced. This is why, when two people fall in love with each other, the impression arises that all your problems have been solved, that all your old oppressions and negative feelings have suddenly disappeared, and that you're completely free of your negative belief and self-rejection. And because of this, you *are* in fact free – for a short time – of the entire ego construction that was responsible for all that distress and self-rejection. This temporary loss of our ego construction during the happiest in-love moments actually brings us very briefly into contact with our natural state, which is pure, clear and full of unconditional love, connectedness and altruism.

Unfortunately, most people completely fail to understand the true origin of those pure feelings of love. After all, the projection mechanism carries on as usual, so you fail to recognise that the other person is merely the trigger of that experience, but instead project the experience onto that other person. As a result, it seems to be the loved one who's so pure and clear and full of unconditional love, and here lies the source of all misery that at later stages ensues from 'falling in love'. You think it's the other person who frees you from your distress and self-rejection, so you become completely dependent on him for sustaining or repeating those short-lived experiences of pure happiness. This experience of unconditional love, which is inherent to your own nature, is immediately made conditional through ignorance of your natural state, and through the projection of that experience onto what triggered it: the loved one. This makes the other person not only the apparent supplier of this deepest happiness, but also the person on whom you become most deeply dependent, and by whom you can therefore feel most deeply rejected. And that rejection will inevitably occur after a while; because it was precisely that latently present rejecting quality that initially made that person so attractive to you. And all this is reciprocal: your lover also fell for your rejecting qualities, when it seemed that you would never reject him. Is it getting too complicated? Then let's look at a real-life example: the relationship of Brett and Gina.

Gina is 35 and has been married to Brett for twelve years. They have two young daughters, aged four and six. She's a sensitive and talented woman, works as a primary school teacher, plays the piano and sings, does meditation and is interested in spirituality. She was a premature baby, and was re-admitted to hospital several times in her early childhood, which meant that she acquired a very basic sense of insecurity. Moreover, her mother had an extremely rejecting and strict parenting style, and was incapable of giving warmth and cuddles and of showing approval. Her father was an emotionally blocked man, who always remained aloof and was no match for his wife's strongly rejecting emotions. Gina's negative belief is 'I am worthless', 'I am weak and dependent' and 'I am a burden to others'. Her main strategy to cover this belief is to try very hard to be good at everything she does, and especially to never be a bother or cause harm to anyone. She has therefore developed a strong image of the cosmopolitan woman, able to successfully juggle the demands of having a busy job and being a mother, wife, daughter and daughter-in-law. In short, she manages pretty well to please everyone, except – of course – herself. At the age of 34 she gets burnout, stops working and becomes depressed.

Brett is 37, a friendly, self-confident, boyish man who has a successful career as a computer specialist and is a fairly accomplished classical guitarist. He comes from a strict Protestant family with a dominant and rejecting father. He often clashed with his father as a child, and every time this happened he was rejected in a very denigrating and hurtful way. His mother was a very warm, sensitive woman, but she herself also suffered from her husband's aggression, and therefore never dared to protect her son from his father. Brett's negative belief is 'I am bad' and 'I don't matter'. His survival strategy is to dissociate from painful feelings, to work very hard at his career, and to put a lot of energy into the good things in life. In addition to working 60 hours a week, he plays in two music ensembles, is an active board member of a tennis club, and has intense contact with his circle of friends. 'Never a dull moment' is his motto: he wants to enjoy life and never again suffer from rejection, restriction or any other complicated stuff. However, he's certainly not a superficial man; on the contrary, he's very interested in other people, a faithful husband, a loyal colleague, and a good friend. It's just that his deeper feelings are very well hidden under layers of pleasant and useful distractions. He fell in love with Gina because of her warmth, her sensitivity and her (apparent) self-sufficiency, but at a deeper level also her extreme dependence, her fear and insecurity. Those qualities made her a safe choice; after all, that dependence would ensure she stayed with him forever.

Gina fell in love with Brett because of his robust independence: his life was arranged exactly as he wanted it, and everything was very well-organised. While she was still in a quandary about a new car or washing machine, he'd already downloaded all the information brochures and within a day a wise choice had been made. With Brett there was nothing complicated, you always knew where you stood with him, he was a tower of strength in her fearful existence.

So you can see that Gina's wish not to be a bother to anyone fitted very well with Brett's wish not to be bothered by anyone ever again. But beneath these dovetailing wishes, the reciprocal rejection already lurked. Brett is attracted to Gina's warm and dependent qualities, because they are the same qualities that his mother had. Brett falls for those qualities because he's dissociated from the warm and dependent qualities in himself. And although his mother let him down in relation to his aggressive father precisely because of those qualities, Gina will never do that, because after all she's dependent on him. In conflicts, dependent mothers always take their husband's side, and hence reject their children. But in your partner, dependence is actually a safe quality: she'll never dare to let you down.

And the other way round, Gina falls for Brett because of his solid autonomy in the world, something that's never developed in herself due to her deep fears and insecurity. However, Brett has become like this because he has permanently suppressed his warm and vulnerable side. In that respect, he's much like Gina's father, who let her down for precisely that reason when she was neglected by her mother. So Brett has the same rejecting qualities as Gina's father, but he'll never let her down: after all, dissociation from his warmth and vulnerability only makes him dependent on Gina, who offers these qualities in abundance.

An important aspect of the situation where two people fall in love with each other is thus the safe 'guarantee' that the other person won't reject you, because that person is dependent on you for something that he or she doesn't have. The missing quality has not developed sufficiently (Gina's independence) or has been largely dissociated (Brett's sensitivity). In general, both partners lack an important ingredient for happiness and independence that the other has to offer. Gina was unable to develop enough security in her early childhood, and Brett offers that. Brett has dissociated from his warm feelings, out of fear of rejection, and Gina can offer that warmth. And she'll never reject him because, after all, she needs his security just as badly. She feels safe with Brett because of his solid personality, but also because he can't live without the warm feelings that he's amputated in himself and that she can give him.

So is the love between two people always such an unconscious horse-trading of security and warmth, you might perhaps wonder? No, in essence there's also something very beautiful going on, but because it's not recognised as such, the horse-trading soon becomes predominant, with all the restrictive consequences of that. We've already seen that the tremendous reciprocal feelings of love and approval temporarily deactivate our deepest self-rejection, so that sometimes the entire edifice of our identity briefly loses its apparent solidity and becomes somewhat transparent. As a result, our deepest and perfect nature – temporarily freed from the covering veil of our self-image – can be more visible and more effective than is usually the case. That's why people who are 'in love' can sometimes appear so radiant. It's also why, when you're in love, you can get such an unusually clear view of what the other is in reality. You fall in love not only with the other person's self-rejecting qualities, but also with what you see behind them. During this in-love phase you can sometimes catch a glimpse of the other person's deepest nature, and that is always worthwhile. Thus Gina saw in Brett not only his solid strength, but also his loving, warm, friendly core, although that hardly ever came to the surface. And Brett saw in Gina not only her warm, vulnerable dependence, but also the promise of a strong, independent, talented woman, although it was never actually fulfilled. Because both partners are unaware of the true nature of their profound and pure feelings, in their relationship they start to do precisely the things that cause the deeper aspects of the other, which they would so dearly like to bring to light, to be buried further and further below layers of self-rejection and protection against each other's rejection. That becomes most clearly visible during the relationship crisis, which will be discussed in the next chapter.

But first take a look at your own experiences with relationships, in the present or in the past. Look at the qualities of your partner that were most attractive to you when the relationship began. Those are qualities that you lack yourself to a greater or lesser extent, because they never developed or because you suppressed them. Also look at situations in which you feel rejected by your partner, or are afraid that this could happen. And then see that there's a connection between what you appreciate in the other and what makes you feel rejected. He appreciates her warmth, vulnerability and dependence, because they give him warmth and security. But he feels misunderstood and obstructed in his need for freedom and for activities without her. She appreciates his strength and stability, but feels let down by his lack of warm, caring emotions, and perceives his need for activities without her as a rejection. Try to see which rejecting quality in your partner was also present in your parents, and how that quality became increasingly evident and annoying during the course of your relationship. And finally, the most difficult analysis of all: can you see that what irritates you most in your partner is a quality that you unconsciously also have yourself, or that you consciously try to eliminate? And if those investigations have made you tired, and you're overcome by a feeling that you've done everything wrong, then don't worry: everyone does it 'wrong', and in the second part of this book you'll see that what is 'wrong' is actually not wrong at all, but a necessary stage on the way to unconditional happiness, with or without a relationship.

11

The relationship crisis

There is hardly any activity, any enterprise, which is started with such tremendous hopes and expectations, and yet, which fails so regularly, as love.

Erich Fromm
German-American philosopher and psychologist
(1900-1980)

You love someone more than words can say. That person also thinks you're the most fantastic and adorable creature in existence. You want to stay together forever, and you're incredibly motivated to make a great success out of being together. 'So what can actually go wrong then?' you would say. And yet things do go wrong with many relationships. In the most painful case, they end in separation or divorce; this is also the most favourable outcome, because at least there's a chance for change and growth. Much more often, they lapse into a dreary kind of 'staying together', not especially lonely but not especially happy either, and always very far removed from that grand ideal of unconditional love and happiness with which the relationship began. Why do things go wrong?

In fact, of course, things are already 'wrong' before we fall in love, simply because we're trapped in a self-image that is aimed solely at keeping us protected from our deepest feelings of worthlessness. In this attempt, falling in love with each other is the best that can be achieved: your most deeply hidden self-rejection temporarily dissolves in your partner's deepest unconditional love. For a short time, you're free of self-rejection and you come into contact with the pure love arising from your natural state. That pure love embraces your partner's most deeply hidden self-rejection, so that she experiences the same thing. Both of you catch a glimpse of the deepest nature of everything, which is usually concealed behind our individual self-image. But because most people don't recognise this essentially spiritual occurrence for what it is, there's immediately a tendency to cling to this beautiful experience, a desire to preserve it and protect it from being lost. You feel a strong motivation to stay together forever and to eliminate anything that could endanger this relationship. Because we didn't recognise the profound happiness as our own inalienable nature, it is projected onto the partner and the relationship, which thus become the greatest good, the most valuable possession that must never be lost. The behaviour that results from this attitude, this protecting and shielding of the relationship, is what ultimately causes it to go wrong.

One of the first symptoms of that mutual dependency is the phenomenon that when you spend some time alone after being with your loved one, having a wonderfully happy time together, you'll soon start to miss her terribly. This is actually a very strange phenomenon. Before you met this person, you felt relatively OK if you were alone. Then you spent some delightfully loving time with her. And after this, when the euphoria has subsided, you suddenly can't feel so OK on your own any more. You miss her, and feel a great need to repeat that wonderful time together. Can you see the similarity to an addictive drug? In that case too, the dependence on the drug only arises after you've been using it. So why is it that having a wonderful time with your loved one has the same addictive effect?

We saw earlier that being so happy together and totally embracing each other's self-rejection brought you very briefly into contact with your natural state, even though this is usually not consciously recognised. As a result, your self-rejection – along with the entire edifice of ways to cover it – temporarily loses its solidity, temporarily becomes slightly transparent, your nature shines through, you are 'radiant' with happiness. But if your identity temporarily loses its solidity, this also means that when the happy time together comes to an end, you're more sensitive to your deep feelings of imperfection and worthlessness, which had previously been safely covered by your identity. These 'withdrawal symptoms' after happy times together are usually not felt as self-rejection; they usually manifest as a strong sensation of needing her, of no longer being able to live without her. We don't recognise this 'need consciousness' as the negative belief, don't feel it as the rejected little child in ourselves, but instead immediately project it onto the loved one: you're no longer able or willing to live without her. And that strong sensation of 'missing' and 'needing' is confused with – and soon replaces – the initial unconditional love arising from the natural state of being. While that initial unconditional love is aimed exclusively at giving love and happiness to the other, the 'needy' love that replaces it is mainly aimed at obtaining reassurance. In this way, expressing 'I can't live without you' feelings is confused with giving love, and the reassuring 'I'll stay with you till death us do part' promises are perceived as receiving love. And this happens on both sides: my neediness is your reassurance, and vice versa. Thus, what is basically a profoundly spiritual occurrence, the reciprocal embracing of the self-rejection, is immediately converted into a reciprocal covering of the self-rejection. The loved one becomes our main supplier of love and approval, and hence the most important part of our self-image. Something that could have helped us become free of that self-image, in fact reinforces it. The game of giving and taking in the market of love and approval reaches its highest point of complexity and refinement in the love relationship. This can go well for a while, and provide a lot of security and satisfaction. But if the perfectly harmonised needs and reassurances start to stagnate anywhere, a relationship crisis immediately ensues, and this delightful game of reciprocal covering changes into a conflict zone of fear and reproach, of hurting the other and protecting yourself from being hurt. Then it indeed turns out that 'love is a battlefield'. But let's look first at how, during the initial phase of the love relationship, the warning signs are set out.

In the first months of the relationship it soon becomes clear where both people's sensitivities lie. What aspects of your loved one's behaviour evoke in you the fear of abandonment or a feeling of neediness? There's no way you can hide this from him or her. For instance, do you start to feel anxious if you haven't heard from your loved one for two days, perhaps disguised as concern for his well-being? Then you'll very soon develop the habit of calling each other every day. Does your lover get anxious if you spend too long chatting with someone else at a party? Then you'll soon start to limit or conceal your contacts with other people. Do you start to doubt whether she loves you if you haven't had sex for a couple of weeks? Then a habitual pattern in relation to sex will soon arise, such as 'once a week, needed or not', or 'whenever the children are staying with their grandparents'. If you dislike your in-laws but your partner thinks you should accompany her to family get-togethers, then you'll soon find a middle way and go with her once in a while. It's possible, of course, that you could also go because you sincerely want to please her, but in that case you're going because you enjoy it. On the other hand, if visiting her family has become a kind of necessary evil to which you submit for the sake of peace and quiet, then it falls into the category of protecting yourself from (the fear of) rejection. The same applies for everything that you either do – or don't do – only because of your partner. Do you go with him to the social evenings at his sports club because he would like you to? Do you go to the ballet with her, even though it bores you to tears? Have you stopped going out for a drink without her because it makes her anxious? Have you stopped singing in a band because he was getting jealous? Have you started doing an evening class because then you can at least be alone occasionally without it causing tensions? Have you stopped working because he thought you should be at home more? Or conversely, do you work a lot of overtime because it's no longer so nice to be at home? Have you stopped going on holiday by yourself, just because you're supposed to go on holiday together? Do you keep quiet about your casual one-nighter, your brief affair or your visit to a sex worker because you can't face all the stress it would cause if she knew? And finally: are you *really* staying together because you just don't want to be alone? Or for the sake of the children?

Those hundreds of big and small concessions and evasions are usually regarded as 'investing in the relationship'. That expression in itself implies that the relationship is something more important than either of the two individuals separately, and that the investment is made with a view to a yield, namely some kind of future security and happiness. In reality, 'investing in the relationship' usually means denying yourself, amputating threatening aspects of your personality, maintaining artificial behaviour, just to avoid confrontation with your needy self, to avoid feeling the fear of rejection, to avoid losing the protective veil that covers the belief that you're worthless or not good enough, which only reinforces that belief, and makes us need the protective veil of the relationship more and more.

In many relationships a situation eventually arises that is very similar to the dependence and restriction that you felt as a child with your parents. Relationships are often a continuation of both the safety and the rejection that you experienced with your parents, an extension of the parent-child restriction in your childhood. You daren't treat each other as adults for fear of losing each other as a safe parent. But that safe parent is also the rejecting parent. In this way, you remain caught between fear of rejection and self-rejection. And the bizarre thing is that the safety for which you give up your autonomy ultimately turns out to be a sham safety, as everyone knows if they've been in a relationship that went wrong: because that safety depends completely on being needed by both partners. As soon as one of them breaks out of that safety, the entire symbiotic mechanism falls apart, with an incredible amount of pain. Let's look at how things went wrong for Brett and Gina.

We've already seen that Gina had to put a tremendous amount of energy into ensuring that she's not a bother to others. At work, she always pushed herself to the limit to make sure she was available to help everyone else, so they wouldn't see that she is '... actually useless and not good enough...' (her own negative belief). But also for Brett, she always does her very best, cooking his favourite meals, going with him for drinks with his work colleagues, to his tennis club parties, his performances with the music ensembles. She does her best to hide her anxiety attacks and feelings of depression from him, or at least not to bother him too much with them. All these exertions result in burnout and depression when she's 34 years old. She increasingly feels a lack of deep feelings of love and companionship in her relationship, sees with increasing clarity how Brett constantly avoids these feelings with his fast and exuberant lifestyle.

For Brett, all this isn't easy: having to look after the children and do the housework more often, when Gina is too tired to do anything at all. He increasingly feels that his love isn't good enough for her. She starts to be manipulative to make him give her more physical warmth and attention. He starts to avoid intimacy with her, because he always feels that he's inadequate in this respect, which is indeed how she perceives it. The frequency of their spontaneous love-making decreases: she feels that he's using her for superficial sex, he feels that his desire for her is rejected, increasingly gets the feeling that she wants something from him that he can't supply. And the relationship drags on like this for years, in a state of ever-increasing oppression and emotional poverty, mainly kept going by a strong sense of duty to the children and that vague feeling of love for each other, love for that deep essence of pureness in the other. However, that love increasingly disappears behind thick layers of neurotic restriction and mutual rejection.

When Brett meets an attractive woman at his tennis club, everything suddenly happens very fast. After all, he's the decisive one who arranges everything so that painful feelings can quickly be resolved. He is completely open about what's going on, right from the start. He tells Gina that he has a new girlfriend and wants to take things further with her. At first, Gina is shocked by this rapid change, but soon she also feels a degree of relief, and even admiration for Brett's decisiveness. She sees that this route offers the only possibility of independence and development. She would never have dared to end the relationship herself, but now that Brett has taken the decision, she gradually feels that a great weight is lifting from her shoulders. After a period of getting accustomed to the new situation, and mourning for the failed relationship, they even start to again feel some mutual respect and friendship for each other as co-parents of their two children.

Thus in every relationship we see a more or less idyllic beginning phase, in which both partners enjoy each other's love and approval, and in which the initial serious disquiet about possible rejection comes to rest, covered with the safe certainty that the other person's need for you is equally strong. The relationship then often goes through a 'honeymoon' phase: the love is still fresh, the security not yet suffocating. After that, very gradually, the rejecting qualities in the partner, which at first were 'seen through the eyes of love' and therefore completely veiled, start to come to the surface. Or in other words: the downsides of your partner's advantages now become evident. The fast, autonomous organiser turns out to be not very good at giving physical warmth and attention. The warm, sweet, motherly woman turns out to be anxious and dependent. The invariably kind man, with whom you never have an argument, increasingly manifests as a wimp. The spirited, articulate, independent woman often changes into a disagreeable harpy.

What actually happens is that the feeling of being 'in love' diminishes, and therefore also the capacity to put a positive spin on everything about the loved one. And it now also becomes increasingly apparent that this love is certainly not unconditional. You start to see more clearly what behaviour is definitely unacceptable in the relationship, on penalty of painful rejection, and what behaviour will result in the desired love and approval. Certain aspects of independent behaviour that you stopped, initially of your own free will, in order to reassure and please him, now turn out to be really forbidden, because they make him feel terribly insecure. At first you might have thought it was nice to send the occasional reassuring text if you were having an evening out without him, but now he gets seriously worried if you go out alone and don't text him. At first you might have enjoyed going with him to his tennis match or choir concert, but at a later stage he sees it as rejection if you decide to stay home instead. While initially you might have shown a keen interest in his explanations about Formula 1 cars or classical music, when he now finds out that really you're not very interested in those subjects, he perceives it as painful rejection. In the early days you might not have mentioned, or have even given up, your habit of getting pleasantly intoxicated in the pub once a month, but now those indulgences are definitely not appreciated, and are guaranteed to cause a cold war in the relationship. And of course the most dangerous minefield of relationships – that is to say: sex – is very soon surrounded by a variety of implicit and explicit warning signs. In almost all love relationships, monogamy is a necessary condition for both partners to feel secure, and anything that might create the slightest hint of unfaithfulness, or the need to be unfaithful, is usually taboo or – if it actually occurs – a source of much pain and rejection, and the most common reason for relationships to fail.

In this 'habituation' phase of the relationship, it turns out that nothing is as addictive as security: the least divergence from the secure routine is regarded as threatening, as a danger to the relationship. In a 'good' relationship, both partners will therefore automatically engage in a more or less serious form of self-amputation: the qualities in me that evoke fear in the other, and will possibly lead to rejection, must be dissociated. If, on the other hand, the partners don't do this, and instead hang on to their 'freedom', the relationship will usually break down at this early stage. It's a painful dilemma, this situation in which you've ended up: either the relationship falls apart, or you have to amputate aspects of yourself.

In this phase we also see all kinds of tricks intended to guarantee the security, and to breathe new life into the daily rut. A lavish wedding can be a celebration of your happiness together, but it is usually also a form of 'sealing the deal' to never reject each other. And in the urban setting there's also another form of sealing the deal: at first, both partners kept their own home, but now they increasingly live together in one of the two places. Then the time comes when it makes more sense to give up the other place, which is hardly used anymore. The cohabitation now receives official status, there's no longer a place where the partners can retreat alone. The relationship's initial openness is now also formally terminated, and it's often not long after this that the first symptoms of the relationship crisis start to show.

The most radical 'sealing' of the reciprocal promise not to reject each other takes place when a baby arrives. Of course it's also an expression of love and togetherness, but the side effect is a strong belief that once there's a child, the partner will never leave. At a later stage of the relationship, this security often results in extra oppression: there's a big taboo on splitting up if you have children, because you don't want to hurt the poor little darlings. The fact that meanwhile the children are seriously weighed down by the tension of a permanent relationship crisis is usually not recognised. It ultimately turns out that children are also only an apparent protection against the failure of the relationship. They can prolong the life of a disintegrating relationship for a while, but they also increase the tension between the partners, so that the relationship eventually breaks up, despite – or even partly because of – the existence of one or more children.

If the relationship survives this phase of sealing the mutual security deal, a more or less stable phase follows. The relationship is perceived as secure, as now beyond all doubt, an unconditional refuge, a symbiosis. Each partner develops his or her non-threatening qualities, and successfully dissociates from threatening qualities. These relationships often have a very clear division of labour: something that one partner is good at will never again be done by the other. The traditional scenario is that he always drives the car, does odd jobs around the house and organises major financial issues like the mortgage and insurance, while she does the caring tasks in the home, has more time for the children and family matters, and deals with the housekeeping. But in the contemporary world, of course, the division of labour can also be entirely different. For the principle, however, this is irrelevant: both partners divest certain complementary aspects of themselves, and together start to form a single, complete, symbiotic entity. And that doesn't only happen in the practical area: he always had difficulty with deeper emotions, that's now her responsibility in the relationship. She always found it difficult to feel safe, that's now his responsibility. In general, we see that the male partner is better at dissociating from unwelcome qualities, and the female partner is better at fully merging with welcome qualities. The 'merged' partner feels unsafe, at the mercy of her own emotions, and is therefore attracted to the 'dissociating' partner, who seems to have his emotions under control. The 'dissociating' partner feels lonely or superficial because of his dissociated emotions, and is therefore attracted by the warmth and depth of the 'merged' partner. A 'good' relationship is thus nothing other than a successful symbiosis of two 'half people'. 'The relationship' becomes the main component of the self-image of both partners, and in many cases even the main purpose to live for.

I just described dissociation and merging as masculine and feminine characteristics respectively. In practice, dissociation is indeed seen more often in men and merging more often in women: for the sake of security in the relationship, women engage most in *doing* and men in *not doing*. Nevertheless, it can also be the case that the woman is the dissociating partner, and the man is the merged one. We then sometimes see relationships where the woman has a 'masculine' role, for example as the breadwinner, and the man has a 'feminine' role, for example as the 'house husband', and they feel very comfortable in those roles. And just to complicate things even further, both partners can be dissociated from one aspect and merged with another aspect. You merge with the qualities from which your partner has dissociated, and you suppress or neglect the qualities with which your partner is merged. Together you form a symbiosis, a whole comprising two half people. And this happens in an identical way in same-sex love relationships, which is why this book doesn't have a separate chapter about gay relationships. There's no difference whatsoever.

Of course you sometimes also see relationships that don't – or only partly – fall into the 'symbiosis trap', and in which both partners also manage to maintain important aspects of their autonomy. For this to happen, however, the partners must make fundamental choices, which aren't always easy, although they create considerably less misery and much more happiness than is possible in the symbiotic relationship. Those choices and non-symbiotic love relationships are what the second part of this book is about.

12

The vicious circle of samsara

With mind far off, not thinking of death's coming,
Performing these meaningless activities,
Returning empty-handed now would be complete confusion;
The need is recognition, the spiritual teachings,
So why not practise the path of wisdom at this very moment?
From the mouths of the saints come these words:
If you do not keep your master's teaching in your heart
Will you not become your own deceiver?

From: The Tibetan Book of the Dead

If the previous chapters have given you the impression that having a relationship is in fact a big trap of pain and misery, then you might now be thinking that this book is advising you to stay – or become – single. But having a love relationship and not having one are two sides of the same coin in the market of love and approval. If you're single, you're usually already creating the conditions for the failure of a relationship you might have in the future. After all, the single life is also aimed at gaining love and approval, even if the 'jackpot' of two people falling in love with each other hasn't been won for a while, or in some cases has actually been carefully avoided. When you're single, you usually have a better distribution of dependencies: you don't depend on the love of just one partner, but nevertheless – like everyone else – you've outsourced your self-esteem to a number of friends, your success at work, contacts with colleagues, interesting hobbies, perhaps a few intoxicants, maybe an occasional short affair, a one-night stand, or a visit to a sex worker. The distress caused by disappointments is possibly less deep, and likewise the happiness in times of success, and the distribution of dependencies makes you more successful at keeping up an appearance of autonomy, in the view of both others and yourself.

As a single person, you always have an opinion about love relationships. Perhaps it's not long since you experienced the painful ending of a relationship, and you're still in a phase of mourning: your self-esteem has taken a bad knock and you frequently feel grief, pain, reproach, frustration, anger or a mixture of these emotions about the break-up of the relationship. Maybe you still have a faint hope that you'll get back together. Or you're throwing yourself into building a new life, starting to do nice things, meet new people; in short, doing everything you can to get new love and approval so the agonising feeling of loneliness and deprivation will go away as soon as possible. And this is precisely where you sow the seeds of a future relationship around falling in love–security–oppression–rejection. It's actually very simple: as long as you're unable *yourself* to integrate your deepest feelings of imperfection and neediness into your spiritual growth, you'll keep making yourself dependent on others to fill that neediness, time after time, and hence will sustain and increase that fundamental misunderstanding of neediness. Thus the way you strive for happiness will constantly obstruct that happiness. The way you try to avoid misery will constantly create new misery.

'Is it really all so terrible? Surely life can also be quite pleasant, right?' You will perhaps object; yes, life is indeed very pleasant, but the way we live it is often counterproductive, often causes unnecessary misery. Maybe you first need to look a bit more closely to really see the painfulness of your situation. This story is definitely not just about the obvious no-hopers, nerds, and losers. It's not only addicts, psychotics, and depressives that hash up their own happiness and cause their own suffering: *everyone* does it. When you look more carefully, you'll see that the most successful businessman feels lonely in his hotel room and is addicted to call girls. You'll see that the stunningly beautiful, world-famous actress always feels insecure and ugly, and goes through one relationship after another. That behind those grand, expensive house fronts in Kensington there are relationships filled with overt or covert despair and reproach. That the world is full of people who safely hide or successfully escape. You'll see that many 'good relationships' are mainly aimed at clinging to a deceptive sense of security and safety. That a single person's non-stop whirlwind of fun activities with friends, exciting theatre shows, and creative hobbies is just one big escape from the fear of being alone with yourself. In short, you'll see that the great happiness that's usually associated with love and approval is almost always either an enticing picture of the future that we crave, or a short-lived wonderful experience that's already become debased in the daily rut of the steady relationship, or a painful memory that we're trying to eradicate with the hope of a new episode of the great happiness.

But perhaps this still sounds rather gloomy and pessimistic to you? I can understand that, and I don't want to deny that there's also happiness in your life, that you might even have quite a nice life. Excellent, there's nothing wrong with that, congratulations! But does it really match up to your highest ideas about happiness? Or have you adapted those ideas to fit 'reality'? You can easily verify this. Check whether you're hoping – consciously or unconsciously – for more happiness and less suffering. Look at whether you're consciously or unconsciously working for an improvement in your position. Do you sometimes think about having a better job, a nicer house, a faster car, a kinder husband, a younger wife? Are you worried about your son's success, your daughter's health, your friend's loyalty, your partner's fidelity, the progress of your career, the development of your talents, other people's recognition of your achievements? And perhaps if your life is *exactly* how you want it to be, then maybe you worry that you don't appreciate it enough, you reproach yourself for being ungrateful, or not being kind enough to other people, or maybe not good enough as a father or mother, friend or partner?

'Yes, but surely all that's quite normal!' you might think. Certainly, it *is* normal in the sense that it's like this for everyone. I'm only trying to show you that it's perhaps not 'normal' that we think this is normal. That it's a symptom of the fundamental misunderstanding. That we're always busy with striving for happiness and avoiding misery, and are never really one hundred percent satisfied. That the way we constantly try to cover the illusion of our own imperfection with other people's love and approval is a vicious merry-go-round into which you're always putting new energy, and which never stops. Until sickness and old age end the rat race, and you have to acknowledge that you've never discovered who and what you really are. Living life on a chest of gold and begging every day, through ignorance: that is our existential situation. Some beggars are perhaps very successful for a while, others less so. But it's true for almost everyone that we live in ignorance of our perfect nature, constantly escaping or covering the frustration that this creates. Are you starting to feel that you'd like to break out of this vicious circle of samsara? To search for the most exciting, fulfilling and happiness-creating insight into your own nature, which is also the nature of everything that exists? Do you like the idea of using relationships for what they essentially are: a way back to our deepest nature? Then I invite you to read the second part of this book, about the spiritual path.

PART 2

Everything is as it is

The Guest House

*This being human is a guest house.
Every morning a new arrival.*

*A joy, a depression, a meanness,
some momentary awareness comes
As an unexpected visitor.*

*Welcome and entertain them all!
Even if they're a crowd of sorrows,
who violently sweep your house
empty of its furniture,
still treat each guest honorably.
He may be clearing you out
for some new delight.*

*The dark thought, the shame, the malice,
meet them at the door laughing,
and invite them in.*

*Be grateful for whoever comes,
because each has been sent
as a guide from beyond.*

Jalaluddin Rumi, Persian poet
(1207-1273) tr. Coleman Barks

13

The spiritual path

The Buddha mind is all-pervasive,
The consciousness of living beings is fragmented.
It is therefore important to develop openness,
As open as the sky.

Sri Simha, Buddhist teacher in India
(8th century)

The most important thing
is to find out
what is the most important thing.

Shunryu Suzuki, Zen master
(1904-1971)

If the first part of this book has got through to you, and you realise that your identity is determined by a vast complexity of misunderstandings, all intertwined and covering each other, you could possibly fall into deep despondency and the feeling that you'll never free yourself from deep-rooted patterns! But don't worry, this reaction is itself part of the problem: it's just another self-rejection and attempt to dissociate from what troubles us; after all, the core of the whole problem is precisely the idea that we need to change something about ourselves in order to become good or worthwhile. The wonderful thing about the spiritual approach is that it doesn't fight the consequences of the misunderstanding, but rather eradicates its cause. It tackles the essence of all problems, namely the mind that both creates and experiences all those problems. If you picture your painful automatic responses as leaves on a tree, then you can certainly try to remove each leaf individually. But really that's an endless task, especially because new leaves grow all the time. The spiritual approach cuts through the roots of the identity tree, causing all the painful leaves to wither and die at once. Although the fundamental misunderstanding may have penetrated into nearly *all* your actions, *all* your thoughts, and *all* your experiences, it's still just one and the same misunderstanding, so the solution is simple: get rid of the misunderstanding.

Buddhism has a good metaphor to clarify this: we all walk barefoot, and this can be painful if we walk on sharp thorns or hard rocks; our usual reaction is to cover those hazards with leather, every hard rock or thorny shrub, so that we don't injure our feet on them. There's simply no end to this. The spiritual approach teaches us that it's more convenient to wear shoes: we recognise that it's our own mind that creates our suffering, and we make sure it stops doing that.

So how is the mind the essence of all our problems? Let's look again at the series of misunderstandings that together constitute our identity. We already saw that our situation is characterised by ignorance of or alienation from our perfect nature. This is the main cause of misery. It sets off a chain reaction of misunderstandings. The mother of all misunderstandings is that we think our nature is imperfect, worthless, or not good enough. This is self-rejection. We then immediately run away from this painful misunderstanding; the mind turns away from its supposed worthlessness, and tries to base a sense of self-esteem on other people's love and approval. This is actually a rejection of our self-rejection, and hence another form of self-rejection.

This gives rise to a complex of patterns and behaviours aimed at getting other people's approval and avoiding their rejection. We then try to hide this entire identity construction behind an image of self-confidence, an 'I have got it all together' show. What the image is trying to hide is a kind of embarrassment about our uncertainty and our dependence on others, so this too is a form of self-rejection.

As our identity grows into adulthood, we merge with safe patterns (fear of rejection) and dissociate from unsafe patterns (self-rejection). Finally we project our dissociated qualities onto other people, whom we then condemn and reject; this too is therefore basically a disguised form of self-rejection.

So you can see that the mother of all misunderstandings, our negative belief, is not only the core of our self-image, but also supplies the energy to all other layers of our identity, and is thus the essence of all other misunderstandings. Self-rejection is the 'spectacles' through which we view all other aspects of our self-image, causing us to be in permanent conflict with ourselves. Take a look at yourself, it's easy to see. Does it sometimes happen that you feel weak or powerless, then you look at yourself and – on top of this – think you're a weakling because you feel weak? Or think you're stupid for thinking that you're stupid? Or get angry with yourself for not controlling your anger? Or hate yourself because you don't love yourself? Every time you become conscious of a painful, distressing, or powerless feeling, it's nearly always a rejecting consciousness. That is the negative belief, the dark-tinted spectacles through which you nearly always view yourself.

The spiritual path gives you insight into this all-pervading misunderstanding, and the means to free yourself from it. To do this, you definitely don't need to engage in a fight against all the misery-creating patterns: fighting against them would only increase the misery, because it would be yet another form of self-rejection. 'Yes, but,' you will perhaps think, 'if you regard everything about yourself as OK, and don't reject it, then nothing's going to change, is it?' But it will, it really will, because change is the nature of all phenomena. Everything changes naturally if you just stop resisting it. It's precisely because you reject them that your self-rejecting patterns are maintained or constantly re-appear in new forms. If you always view your self-rejection with a self-rejecting eye, how will you ever be able to end your self-rejection? It's only if, instead of this, you develop a kind and open awareness of yourself that the usual tensing-up reaction dissolves, and everything changes in a natural way. This means that everything changes in accordance with your nature, which is already perfect. It's self-rejection that prevents us from seeing that perfect nature. It's self-rejection that prevents us from recognising and letting go of our desperate striving for other people's love and approval. It's self-rejection that prevents us from letting go of our hardened image of self-confidence and self-protection. It's self-rejection that, time after time, makes us dissociate from painful patterns and feelings, which in fact only sustains them.

But note carefully: stopping your self-rejection is not the same as resigning yourself to your feelings of worthlessness; that would be more of a victim role, likely to result in depression. Neither is it convincing yourself that you're good by nature; that would be more of a New Age belief, which would only temporarily cover your self-rejection. Stopping your self-rejection is like removing the dark-tinted spectacles and starting to look at and recognise who you really are.

Another way to explain this is to use the word 'aversion' instead of 'self-rejection'. Ignorance of our perfect state of being causes aversion to our supposed imperfect nature, our negative belief. This gives rise to attachment to other people's love and approval, as the means to cover that imperfect nature. But we also feel aversion to the fundamental insecurity and artificiality of those covers, so attachment to the cover of the cover arises: we hide our dependency and insecurity, the 'inner self-image', behind an image of self-confidence, an 'ideal self-image'. And each time when, after a while, we become aware of a certain aspect of that attachment (merging), we immediately feel aversion again, and have the tendency to dissociate from that pattern and merge with an alternative form of self-protection, a new 'ideal self-image'. It is thus through our aversion and our attachment to its cover that our suffering is maintained (see Figure 3).

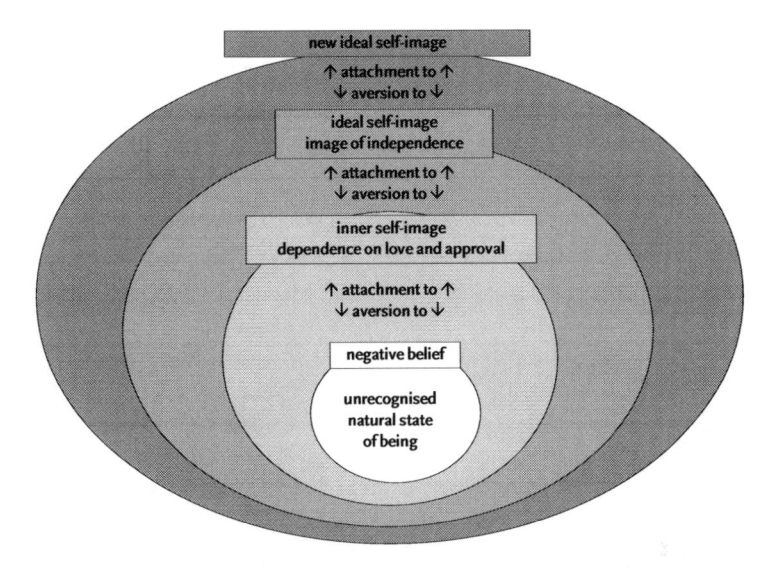

Figure 3: Aversion to a feeling or pattern (dissociation) also causes attachment to the cover of that feeling or pattern (merging).

Can you see that aversion or self-rejection is the engine behind all problems? Which is excellent news, because self-rejection is something that you do yourself; so you can learn to stop doing it! The opposite of self-rejection and aversion is allowing, embracing, integrating. How wonderful it is to see that *this* is the solution: allowing. You don't have to change or improve everything first, because that would be a never-ending endeavour. Simply allowing, softening, opening is the solution. Kindness instead of aversion; self-approval instead of self-rejection.

The spiritual path consists of practises and strategies that enable you to develop this kindness towards yourself. But something you won't find in this book is a set of instructions on how to start loving yourself: because loving yourself can only arise spontaneously when you learn to stop rejecting yourself. If you *do* try to love yourself as a strategy to get rid of your problems, it will soon become a trick to get rid of unpleasant feelings. And that is a form of dissociation, and therefore doomed to create more misery than it eliminates. Moreover, truly loving yourself is definitely not just a nice feeling of being worthwhile; it's an all-pervasive understanding that you're worthwhile regardless of how good or how worthless you feel.

Stopping self-rejection is thus the simplest solution for all our problems. And self-rejection was, in turn, the consequence of not recognising our perfect nature. So stopping self-rejection and realising our perfect nature are actually two aspects of the same spiritual process. Because that is ultimately the essence of every spiritual path: discovering the true state of being, the real nature of all phenomena, and hence also of one phenomenon in particular: myself and my mind. As the Tibetan Buddhist master Tulku Urgyen (1920-1996) says:

Samara is mind turned outwardly, lost in its projections;
*Nirvana is mind turned inwardly, recognising its nature.**

This reversal of the mind's direction is a crucial feature of every spiritual path. You can spend all day reciting mantras, trance-dancing, praying to God or Allah, twisting yourself into the most difficult yoga positions, helping other people or reading inspirational books and going to workshops, but if you don't turn your mind around to search for its own deepest nature, you're not on a spiritual path in the most profound sense of the expression. You might engage in religious pursuits, or ethical, altruistic or charitable activities, and these can all be very useful, but they only become spiritual when they're directed towards ending your alienation from your own nature.

However, all kinds of things can go wrong here, so that our attempts to achieve spiritual growth actually hinder that growth. The same counterproductive mechanism that led to the creation of our oppressive identity can also kick in when we try to free ourselves from it. For example, we can again start to see our self-rejection as an

---

* *Samsara* is Sanskrit for 'cycle' or 'wandering'. *Nirvana* is the term used for 'enlightenment', but its literal meaning in Sanskrit is 'extinguishing': namely, of the causes of samsara.

enemy that must be conquered. We can regard our identity, our ego, as the big villain that must be eliminated. We can view the pleasant feelings that result from less self-rejection as an end in themselves, and then develop a new attachment to them. In short, whatever *can* go wrong will certainly *go* wrong from time to time, and when we recognise and don't reject this, all our mistakes are converted into steps forward on the spiritual path.

The spiritual path has two approaches: the relative and the absolute. The relative approach involves learning to see through all the painful automatic responses in your self-image, desisting from the self-rejection within them, and developing positive automatic responses instead. This approach is very practical, requires a lot of effort and targeted training, and will slowly but surely yield a reduction in misery and an increase in happiness.

The absolute approach aims directly at ending the main cause of the whole series of misunderstandings: ignorance of our perfect nature. This approach is difficult to describe in words; it brings you into direct contact with your natural state, and can only be learned from a spiritual friend or teacher. You might be inclined to think that the latter approach is more appealing, but in fact they are both necessary; one isn't possible without the other. It's true that via the absolute approach you can catch glimpses of your perfect nature in a very short time, but – however inspiring that may be – the influence of your negative automatic responses will cause you to lose those experiences just as quickly. On the other hand, you can try to end all your destructive automatic responses one by one and replace them with positive responses, but if you aren't inspired by the recognition of your perfect nature as you do this, it will be a very long road indeed.

There are teachers today who extol the absolute method as the only true way. Their message is that you already *are* enlightened, but you just don't see it yet. You don't need to do anything, change anything, train anything. Everything is already perfect, all you have to do is allow this to enter your mind. All spiritual training is superfluous, they say, and even holds you back from realising your enlightened state. Funnily enough, at an absolute level they're quite right. Unfortunately, that absolute level isn't realised by most people, and regardless of how often you say it exists, spontaneous realisation occurs in only one or two rare individuals. The others, such as ourselves, will still need to follow a relative approach. Only then will your negative automatic responses become weaker, and will there be space to reverse the direction of your mind and learn to recognise your own perfect nature. Only by combining the relative and absolute approaches will you ever reach the point from where you can see that you were always already enlightened, and that everything was already perfect.

In the relative approach to the spiritual path, one can roughly distinguish three main schools, which in Buddhism are called *hinayana*, *mahayana* and *vajrayana*. They contain a wonderfully rich spectrum of knowledge and methods for spiritual growth and realisation, more than enough for an entire lifetime's study. But they can also be essentially summarised as three strategies that can be used separately or together, depending on the situation. The hinayana strategy teaches you to avoid or eliminate situations and thoughts that cause misery: what we referred to earlier as the 'triggers'. This strategy involves trying to end your destructive habits, such as addictions or self-neglect, and situations where you feel very distressed or inflict harm on others. It creates more peace in your life, more simplicity, less stress, and therefore also less escape behaviour, for instance in alcohol, drugs, or watching TV. It doesn't necessarily entail asceticism, and enjoyment of the good things in life is still recommended.

The mahayana strategy aims at the development of positive automatic responses as an antidote to the negative ones. So not only desisting from self-destruction, but at the same time starting to develop automatic responses that are positive for yourself and others. In the mahayana strategy you change your 'need consciousness', which makes you always require other people for love and approval, into a kind of 'abundance consciousness', which allows you to give love and approval to all beings, including yourself. In this strategy, you practise loving kindness as the antidote to your former tendency towards aversion and (self)rejection. You develop insight into the changeable nature of all circumstances as the antidote to your tendency to cling to pleasant things. You become increasingly aware of the mutual dependency of all phenomena as the antidote to moral dogmatism and your tendency to condemn others and yourself. In reality, there is no good and evil, just actions that lead to more happiness or more misery for yourself and others.

The vajrayana strategy doesn't avoid anything, and doesn't use an antidote method to convert negative patterns into positive ones, but aims at recognising the pure essence in all negative patterns. In this approach, emotions that are usually regarded as negative, such as aggression and obsession, aversion and attachment, are therefore not avoided or neutralised, but are completely seen through and 'felt through', and transformed into their pure essence. This converts every form of aversion into clarity, and every form of attachment into warmth and love. And those are precisely the basic qualities of our natural state of being: clarity and love.

You can apply these three strategies to every problematic situation. In a serious relationship crisis, for example, you can decide to live apart for a while to give yourself and each other some peace and space. That is the hinayana method. But at the same time you can engage in relationship therapy to help improve communication with each other and recognise negative automatic responses and replace them with positive ones. That is the mahayana method. If you additionally take full responsibility for all your painful feelings, and through contemplation and meditation transform them into love and clarity, then you are using the vajrayana method. This can be summarised even more simply:

1 try to end negative and destructive patterns (hinayana method)
2 develop positive, happiness-creating patterns (mahayana method)
3 reverse the direction of your mind towards its own perfect nature (vajrayana method)

The following chapters contain concrete elaborations of these spiritual principles, and describe how you can free yourself from self-rejection, in both your relationship with yourself and your love relationships. In all this, you should never forget that spiritual knowledge isn't intended to be accepted without question, but rather is intended as an invitation to investigate its truth for yourself. How to do this is also part of that spiritual knowledge. Some of the knowledge will perhaps appeal to you and inspire you to do research. Other knowledge will maybe leave you cold or will even repel you, and then it's best to just leave it aside as (perhaps temporarily) unusable.

There's a Zen story about a spiritual trainee who was so full of his own ideas that his master was finding it impossible to teach him anything new. One day the master asked the trainee, 'Would you like another cup of tea?' But the trainee hadn't even started on his first cup, so he politely refused. The master then picked up the teapot and began to pour tea into the full cup. The tea overflowed onto the table and the trainee's robe. 'Hey, what are you doing?' he yelled in surprise. The master replied, 'It's the same with your mind: it's so full that there's no room at all for any new insights.'

14

Letting go of 'relationship thinking'

The real voyage of discovery consists not in seeking new landscapes but in seeing with new eyes.

Marcel Proust, French writer
(1871-1922)

Once you've figured out that your self-image is mostly determined by your dependence on love and approval, and you know that the love relationship is where the reciprocal exchange of these reaches its absolute zenith, you'll hardly be surprised that having – or not having – a love relationship plays an important part in our thinking. For many people, the love relationship is the ultimate goal in their life, because they're either trying to get a relationship if they don't have one, or they're hanging on to it if they do. And in some people, after a series of painful experiences, we sometimes see the opposite reaction: never wanting another relationship again then becomes their most important perspective on life. Both attitudes are symptoms of 'relationship thinking'. If you're giving serious consideration to creating more happiness and harmony in your life, the best way to start is to let go of this relationship thinking, and take a spiritual perspective. This involves acknowledging that striving for other people's love and approval is the cause of a vast amount of suffering and at best can bring happiness only temporarily; and conversely the realisation of your perfect natural state will result in unconditional and supreme happiness. An expression that's currently popular in this context is 'having a good relationship with yourself', and this metaphor can certainly be useful for a while, until you discover that in this natural state there's no distinction any more between your relationship with yourself and your relationship with others.

Letting go of relationship thinking therefore means that you no longer regard having or not having a relationship as your goal in life, but see it as a circumstance which you do or don't encounter, and which you can learn from and enjoy for as long as it lasts. Relationship thinking suggests that a 'good relationship' is final and permanent; that is to say, 'till death us do part'. In reality, nothing is final and permanent, and thinking that a relationship is, or should be, just makes us cling to it desperately and feel tremendous pain if the relationship consequently goes wrong.

In our society, relationship thinking is established as completely natural. When we read about the number of marriages that end in divorce (around 30%), it's often said that this is a high percentage, and that it's an undesirable phenomenon (sometimes making reference to the past, when the percentage was lower). But once you've seen through relationship thinking, you understand that divorces aren't actually a cause for concern, and the problems associated with them are due to the misconception that they shouldn't be allowed to occur. We've already seen that most traditional love relationships are more or less a continuation of the dependency and safety of the parental family. This is why, for many people, the break-up of a relationship represents a step forward towards adulthood. We also see that relationships that start when the partners are older, and have both had previous relationships, sometimes place less emphasis on that mutual dependency, and leave more space for individual development. Of course there are also people who, as soon as one relationship breaks up, immediately take their neurotic problems with them into the next one. In that case, the change of relationship is entirely about dissociation from painful feelings; or to put it simply, it's an escape from the current problems to new problems in the future. Be that as it may, having a happy relationship is something you can learn (and so too is being happy if you *don't* have a relationship), and the experience of one or more broken relationships can contribute greatly to that learning process.

It's not really surprising that relationship thinking is so widely established: it's a direct derivative of the 'need consciousness' that almost everyone has; the deep feeling that you're basically imperfect, not complete, not good enough (the negative belief), plus the strong urge to cover that feeling with other people's love and approval. The only way to really get rid of that need consciousness is to realise your perfect nature. But that will never happen if your striving continues to be aimed exclusively at gaining other people's love and approval. You must therefore start by letting go of relationship thinking. But note carefully: this does not mean that you must make yourself stop doing it! That wouldn't even be possible, because in fact you never consciously started doing it; rather, it just happened to you through the influence of ignorance and circumstances. Becoming free of relationship thinking occurs naturally when you learn to recognise its symptoms in yourself, and to accept them with kind awareness. Neither does it mean that you can never start another relationship, or have to end your current one. It simply means that you examine the way in which you cling to relationship thinking, and then embrace the results of that examination with kind awareness; that is to say, without judgement.

If you're in a relationship, imagine that one day your partner tells you that he'd really love to go travelling alone for a year. Or that she wants to spend a year on retreat with a spiritual master high in the Himalayas. Just try to feel what your reaction would be. Don't judge those feelings. Maybe you can identify fear of losing your partner, anger at such a stupid plan, or reproach because your partner is abandoning you. Maybe you also feel self-rejection because of those feelings, you'd prefer to be generous and not begrudge your partner this opportunity. Or you feel highly indignant: your partner has really got it wrong, you just don't do something like that if you love each other!

For a moment, don't look at the practical consequences of the plan, but at your tendency to treat your partner like a child and keep him tied down or conversely push him away. Look at your tendency to make the other person responsible for your painful feelings.

When you've let go of relationship thinking, there's first and foremost a strong understanding that you have no right to the other person, and that you're also neither able nor willing to forbid him anything. This doesn't alter the fact that, in the above example, you perhaps feel rejected or abandoned, and are afraid of losing your partner. Those feelings are perfectly normal and are not the real problem. That problem only arises if you hold the other person responsible for those feelings. Then you make yourself a victim, no longer able to do anything except manipulate your partner until he or she stops doing what's causing your pain. The other person feels this as rejection, and tries to manipulate you. The consequence is that both of you become distressed. All this misery is avoided if you take responsibility yourself for everything that you feel. And it's also only then that you can use your painful feelings on the spiritual path and give your partner the space to go his own way. It's possible that in the above example the relationship will break up, or after a year of voluntary separation will actually blossom with even more love and gratitude on both sides. In either case, one can see growth, a big step towards becoming free of the 'need consciousness', and towards realisation of your natural state of being.

Within a traditional relationship you probably won't even voice such a wish to spend a year apart, and will dismiss it in advance as bad, selfish, and against the relationship rule that you must always stay together. And if your wish is actually put into words, in most cases it will cause lots of trouble and – if you persist with it – a painful break-up of the relationship. Not because of the plan itself, but because of the reaction of the partners, who hold each other responsible for the distressed or fearful feelings that result from it. You see, if you really think the other person is responsible for your deep feelings of fear and rejection, then in the long run there's nothing you can do except end the relationship. How much more love and space is possible in a relationship where the partners take responsibility *themselves* for their feelings! If you get really good at this, there will in fact never again be a reason not to love the other person. The form of the relationship can and will change over time, but the love that springs directly from your natural state is enduring. Here too, then, the counterproductive paradox is evident: if you cling to your relationship as a lifelong guarantee of security, your love constantly runs into problems. But if you recognise that relationships are temporary and changeable, your love endures.

You can also do a similar 'thought experiment' if you aren't in a relationship. Just look at how the longing for a fulfilling love relationship is present in your mind. Imagine that for the rest of your life you'll never have such a relationship. See yourself when you're old, on your own in a little house or care home, without a life partner, without someone you love. What feelings arise? Fear of loneliness and death? Resistance to this painful idea? What exactly do you miss most in this picture of a future without a relationship? The togetherness? The love? Good sex? Security? Self-esteem? Happiness?

So you can see that we more or less link all the good things in life to having a love relationship. No wonder we feel scared about not having one or losing one. But in reality it's possible to experience love, happiness, security, self-esteem, and even good sex without a love relationship. When your need consciousness is transformed into an abundance consciousness, you live permanently in a state of love, and you effortlessly give love to others, regardless of whether or not you have a love partner.

Do you think it seems a good idea to let go of your need consciousness and aim for an abundance consciousness arising from your natural state? For a moment, don't think of all the frightening consequences, because *that* is the need consciousness resisting its own abolition. Just look at the hopelessness of relationship thinking, how it constantly holds out the promise of eternal happiness with your lover, making you always remain dependent, afraid of rejection, striving for future happiness and meanwhile repeatedly losing yourself, always needy for other people's love and approval, never in contact with who you really are. Take time to let the choice that you're now facing really sink in. Look at how wonderful it is that you're curious about the deeper layers of your existence, and are discovering that there is indeed a choice for a happier and more meaningful existence.

Look also at how quickly your life goes by: if you don't make a choice, you actually choose to waste your time. Don't keep waiting and hoping that someone will come along to bring you the great happiness that in reality you already have within you. Recognise that the only way out of the miserable vicious circle of misunderstandings is to choose in favour of your own perfect nature. See how your life has been hurtling along on the same track for years. Have you already noticed how hard it is to really take a different route? Perhaps you've been inspired for some time by certain ideas or books or teachers, but have never succeeded in really changing the way you live your life. That's because the need consciousness is afraid of this choice, and tells you that you'll have to give up all your comfort and luxury and security. But that's a distortion of reality, seen through those need-tinted spectacles. In reality, you'll eventually start to find comfort less important, because you already feel comfortable enough. You'll cling less to secure situations, because you feel secure enough in yourself. In short, letting go of your need consciousness is only scary as long as you're still thinking about it. Once you make the decision, it will be the most important, most profound and most joyful choice you've ever made. You've chosen the spiritual path towards your own deepest nature, which is also the nature of everyone and everything.

15

Looking at your own mind: who is looking?

Spring morning on the lake:
The wind merges with the rain,
Worldly matters are like flowers
That fall only to bloom again.
I retire to contemplate behind closed doors,
A place of true joy,
While the floating clouds come and go
The whole day long.

Zhengue, Zen master
(12th century)

Choosing to take the spiritual path therefore involves letting go of relationship thinking. Relationship thinking arises out of the 'need consciousness', which in turn is the consequence of self-rejection. Stopping self-rejection corresponds to realising your perfect nature. From this realisation, there arises an 'abundance consciousness'.

Once you've made the fundamental choice in favour of your perfect nature, the most important consequence will follow naturally, and that is practis. Turning the direction of your mind back towards its own perfect nature requires training. After all, you've spent your whole life practising how to run away from your own nature, because of the misunderstanding that it's inadequate and inferior. Those escape mechanisms are quite ingrained by now, and you'll need to practise in order to unlearn them. The spiritual path offers a wide range of methods, so your training can always be attuned to your individual requirements. In this book you'll find a few of those methods, and we'll start with the most important one, which is also the basis of all other methods: learning to look at the essence of your own mind.

Your mind is a busy chatterbox, producing a constant stream of thoughts, always one at a time, one after the other, long sequences that together form a story, creating new stories or going around and around in old familiar stories. Those stories are about reality, or more precisely, they completely determine our perception of reality. If you try to fight them, or try not to think certain thoughts, they just get stronger. If you try to stop the mind, it just gets busier and slides away in all directions. This is what we call the conceptual or thinking mind.

The above description doesn't tell you anything new, you already knew this. How? Because you not only have a thinking mind, but also an awareness of that thinking mind, otherwise you wouldn't know your own thoughts. This aware mind is permanently present, even while you're reading this. Think about it: you know what you're reading now while you're reading. What is it that's reading along with you and knows what you're reading, and right now even knows that you know what you're reading? Now read a bit more, as you allow the awareness 'I am reading' to sink in. Are you aware right now that you're reading this sentence? Can you see that this awareness is always there, and that usually you're not conscious of it? But because you're now briefly conscious that you're reading this, this permanent awareness becomes briefly conscious of itself. This 'self-conscious' awareness is the essence of the mind. Now stop reading and stay in this self-aware awareness for a few seconds...

You'll notice that it's not long before this self-knowing awareness loses itself again in a new series of thoughts. Even then, there's still awareness, but it's no longer conscious of itself, it loses itself in a stream of thoughts or events. So how do you know it's still there? Because otherwise you wouldn't know about your thoughts; you'd be like a computer. A computer can also observe if you connect a camera to it, and hear if you connect a microphone to it. A computer can think if you get it to execute a process, and can remember the results. But whatever the computer does, it doesn't *know* that it's doing it, there's no consciousness, no awareness of its own existence. Just like a computer, our mind can observe, listen, execute, and remember mental processes, but throughout all this, in addition, it permanently has a conscious quality. That is the essence of the mind. We're usually not conscious of that conscious or 'knowing' quality. The awareness has lost itself and is carried along in the stream of thoughts. But if you want to, or if you're reminded of it, you can bring that awareness back into contact with itself.

The name that we usually give to this everyday awareness, which has lost itself and is swept along by the stream of thoughts, is 'consciousness'. It's present the whole day long, even when you're dreaming and even slightly during your dreamless sleep. After all, if a loud noise occurs while you're asleep, it evidently penetrates to your consciousness: it wakes you up. It's only after suffering a severe impact to the head that you can temporarily be truly 'unconscious'.

When this consciousness is conscious of itself, we call it 'awareness'. The terms 'consciousness' and 'awareness' are fairly arbitrary and serve only to avoid confusion. It's more important that you recognise the distinction between those two forms of being. In everything that you do, consciousness is present without being noticed. But if you're reminded of it, and you allow your mind to be conscious of itself, then for a moment there is awareness. Take a look for yourself, then I'll show you once again. Right now, you're reading this sentence. Can you read this sentence and at the same time be aware that you're reading it? Do you see that you then briefly go into a kind of clarity, not only of your mind but simultaneously also of a 'here-and-now feeling'? Can you feel the 'here-and-now space' around you? Right now, are you very briefly conscious of your consciousness? That's your awareness, the self-knowing essence of the mind. It's very subtle and disappears again as soon as it has 'touched' itself. But you can also repeatedly evoke it: consciousness of your consciousness, awareness, consciously 'being'. Do you see that it's clear and open, and perfectly free from judging and rejecting? It can embrace everything.

When your consciousness is conscious of itself, it doesn't mean that everything else disappears. You still see with your eyes, you still hear with your ears, you have feelings, thoughts arise, but in all this there is also briefly that 'knowing' quality, that awareness that is free from judgement and rejection. And a moment later it's gone again, you're again being swept along in your stream of thoughts; you *are* your stream of thoughts.

How do you know that the awareness is free from judgement and rejection? Because they take place in the thinking mind; while you're judging or rejecting you can *know* that you're judging or rejecting. That is the awareness of the judging or rejecting, which itself is therefore free from judging or rejecting.

The awareness is sometimes known as the 'witness', because it constantly witnesses everything that occurs in your mind and around you. That 'witness' is never affected by what occurs in your mind, just like a mirror does not become dirty by the objects that it reflects. Awareness is always pure, clean, and clear. It is the essence of the mind. Can you see that each time your consciousness is conscious of itself, it is the mind that looks at its own essence? Try to observe that essence. Can you see that it's the mind that is trying to observe itself? Have you spent years searching for your 'soul', your 'Buddha nature', the 'meaning of life' or your 'natural state of being'? Then turn around and look at your searching mind. Although I should just say that you won't actually find 'something' when you look at that searcher; the mind isn't a 'thing' that you can point to. It can best be compared to an open, unbounded space. That is awareness: open, unbounded space, witnessing everything that happens in that space: thoughts, feelings, perceptions.

That spacious, aware mind usually loses itself in a stream of thoughts, feelings, and events. It has then identified itself with the stream of thoughts, and it also experiences temporary joys and sorrows of this. But you can de-identify yourself from that oppressive identity. Let the mind be conscious of itself; rest in that open space of the self-aware mind. You'll notice that each time you can only stay in that awareness very briefly, before it loses itself again in a stream of thoughts or events. With practise, you learn to gradually extend those moments, and can stay in the aware state more often and for longer. As a result, that state becomes progressively clearer and more loving, which then makes it easier to stay in it for longer. Ultimately you achieve an effortless state of permanent awareness. That is the definitive end of your suffering.

In order to realise this effortless natural state of being, the spiritual path offers a wealth of different practises. Many of these are aimed at quietening the mind. If your mind is very wild and constantly leaps back and forth between all kinds of stories about reality, about the past or the future, then it's almost impossible to make it change direction and look at its own essence. This is why it first has to be calmed a little. These quietening practises are summarised by the term *shamata*, which is Sanskrit for 'calm abiding'. It's a form of training in focusing your attention.

There is, incidentally, a slight difference between attention and awareness. Awareness is the mind that is conscious of itself. Attention is the mind that is focused on one object. There are two kinds of attention: spontaneous attention and controlled attention. If you're listening to a beautiful piece of music, or watching an exciting movie, your mind is focused very attentively on that object. This happens spontaneously because you find the music beautiful or the movie exciting. You don't have to make any effort for this. And when the music or movie comes to an end, your mind will automatically go back to other objects. In fact, your attention flies back and forth for the whole day between what you see and hear, and think and feel, without you having much influence on it. This can sometimes cause you to become very agitated.

In the practice of shamata, you focus the mind on an object that in itself isn't especially attractive, and try to keep your attention on that object for some time. This is controlled attention. You can use a stone or a flower, or a picture of a Buddha, a candle or a piece of crystal, anything at all. Try looking attentively for a while at a completely uninteresting object, such as a chair or cupboard in your room.

You'll soon notice that your mind doesn't like this and constantly slides away to more interesting objects, thoughts about the past or the future, or things that are happening around you. You'll also notice that you can feel a mild form of frustration about this: you're not the master of your own mind, and it's not pleasant to discover this. There are spiritual traditions that turn this practice into a battle for total control over your own mind. If you practise very hard for years, it can indeed be achieved. But although this results in a calm mind, it still isn't a mind that recognises its own nature. This is why I suggest a different approach here, where you don't need to have total control over your mind, but instead can make friends with it. In this approach, you simultaneously train both your attention and your awareness. I'll first explain the physical posture of this method, and then the mental attitude.

The physical posture for this practice is characterised by a combination of relaxation and alertness. You sit on a cushion, with your legs crossed or in lotus position, or simply on a chair. It doesn't really matter, as long as you sit comfortably and with a straight back. Your head upright, your shoulders relaxed, your hands resting on your legs, or folded in your lap. The most important thing is that you're relaxed as you sit, but with a straight back so that you also remain attentive and alert.

In this method you must learn to practise with your eyes open. There are many meditation methods where you close your eyes, but they aim solely at quietening the mind by shutting yourself off from distraction around you. This method places emphasis on seeing your own mind with increasing clarity, and for this it's best to get used to keeping your eyes open.

The mental attitude during this practise is also relaxed and alert. You bring your attention very gently to an object. You can use a flower or a stone, for example, but the best object is your own breathing. Look at the expansion and contraction of your abdomen with every breath, or at the feeling of the air as it flows through your nose or throat. Try to focus your attention very gently on your breathing, without concentrating or forcing yourself, and without shutting yourself off. At the same time, stay very openly and spaciously present with everything that happens in your mind and around you. See thoughts arising, hear sounds around you, let everything be there, but try to always keep a bit of attention on your breathing. And throughout all of this, try to remain constantly conscious of your own mind; *know* that you're doing this. While you're inhaling, know that you're inhaling; while you're exhaling, know that you're exhaling.

You'll notice that you repeatedly get distracted by your own stream of thoughts, and that you have the tendency to condemn this. But this is precisely part of the practise! There's nothing you can do about your mind repeatedly getting distracted by thoughts or events. What you're therefore actually practising here is to refrain from judging the fact that it repeatedly gets distracted. In this way, you make friends with your own mind. Each time you notice you were distracted, this is – in itself – the end of being distracted, and you can bring your attention back to your breathing. The practise thus involves the following successive phases: you're attentive and aware, then you become distracted without noticing it, a little later you notice you were distracted and try not to judge it, and finally you bring your attention back to your breathing and your awareness back to itself. You go through these phases time and time again.

If you look very carefully, you'll see that our deep-rooted tendency towards merging or dissociation has its origins in this cycle. Each time your mind gets distracted by the stream of thoughts without you noticing it, a subtle form of merging with the contents of your mind takes place. And each time you become conscious of this and notice that you were distracted, there is the condemnation, the tendency to dissociate from that busy and distracting stream of thoughts.

It can be helpful here to congratulate yourself each time you notice that you were distracted. Because that moment is the minuscule precursor of total enlightenment: the distracted mind that suddenly finds itself again. They are all actually moments of joy and clarity, if you look closely.

Can you see how the basis of our veiled mind is revealed by meditation? By practising kind awareness instead of remaining merged with your stream of thoughts, or dissociating from it, the cause of all painful identity patterns is dissolved at the root. Look at how this works in everyday life, for instance, if you're worrying about a problematic situation. Occasionally there's a moment when you become conscious of your worrying. This consciousness will immediately be coloured by self-rejection and result in an unpleasant feeling. You'll want to get rid of that feeling, so your mind will automatically start to think even more about a possible way out of the problem. So you go around and around worrying about a problem. But when you have some experience with meditation, those moments of consciousness during the worrying actually offer you the way out: instead of rejecting and dissociating, you continue to look at yourself and your worrying with kind and non-judgemental awareness. As a result, the worrying is no longer fuelled by rejection, and after a while will naturally resolve itself.

A very significant trap into which everyone who meditates falls from time to time is to deliberately strive for a calm mind. This striving arises through your aversion to a busy mind and your attachment to a calm mind, and is therefore a form of dissociation. And it also doesn't help at all: it just makes the mind even busier. During meditation the mind will sometimes naturally become calmer. That's a pleasant experience and you can certainly enjoy it, as long as you don't then start trying to strive for that calmness.

While practising, you'll quite often find that your mind jumps around like a puppy, and all you feel is disquiet. This isn't wrong; in fact, it's quite the opposite! This is the true practise: being able to stay present with a busy, agitated, or irritated mind! You'll notice that at first you feel a strong tendency to value and strive for the calm mind, and to condemn and suppress the busy, agitated mind. This is therefore the most subtle form of our tendency to merge with what we like and to dissociate from what we don't like, and is therefore in fact the essence of self-rejection, which is why this practise, at the deepest level, changes your tendency towards self-rejection into an attitude of kindness to your own mind, regardless of its contents. And the wonderful thing is it ultimately turns out that a kind and aware mind is, in itself, also a calm mind. So for this you mustn't fight the busy mind, but must learn to embrace it with attention and awareness. That is the essence of meditation.

Meditation is the greatest and most beautiful gift you can give yourself. Just by practising, you can develop a kind, calm mind and thus realise the effortless natural state of being. Just by practising, you can teach the mind to stop rejecting itself and instead learn to see its own deepest essence. Just by practising, you can end your self-rejection, see through your oppressive identity, and free yourself from dependence on other people's love and approval. Just by practising, practising, and practising.

This might sound like a tiresome and difficult chore which, although will eventually yield a wonderful result, will involve years and years of extra work. But that's absolutely not how it is. As soon as you start to practise, you'll notice that you will enjoy it, and that it will become more enjoyable. Quite soon you'll notice that your mind becomes calmer, kinder, and clearer, while painful and distressing emotions gradually becomes less painful and distressing. And you certainly don't need to start by meditating for two hours a day; in fact, that wouldn't be a good idea at all! It's best to start with five minutes a day, preferably at the same time each day. The earlier in the day the better, as it will soon affect your mind during the day. Create a place in your home where you can be alone and undisturbed; make it comfortable, arrange some objects that inspire you, such as photos of your loved ones, or of people who give you inspiration, a candle, a flower, a small Buddha statue, whatever you like. Anything is permitted if it helps you to feel 'at home'. And then, just do it; simply sit and look at your own mind. You'll soon find that it becomes a safe place of refuge in your life, a place where – for a moment – nothing at all is required of you.

I should also mention, however, that you'll soon become familiar with a very strange phenomenon: when you're doing the practise you'll really enjoy it, but when you *think* about it beforehand, your mind will protest and won't want to start. The reason is that the ordinary, everyday, busy mind absolutely doesn't want to look at itself, because it dislikes itself and would prefer to be distracted, to experience nice exciting things, and focus on other people's love and approval. So if you think too much about whether or not to meditate, you'll never get around to it. At the beginning, you have to outsmart your self-rejecting mind by not thinking about it but just sitting down and doing it, every day. After a while you'll be accustomed to this and will never want to miss these precious moments with yourself. So make a plan. Decide when, where, and for how long you're going to sit every day to do your practise. Create a suitable place. Think in advance what practise you want to do and what you need for it. Some people like to write down a few inspiring quotations on a card and read them during the practise. Or to read a page of an inspiring book and then immediately meditate for five minutes. Learn to inspire yourself with whatever resources you find helpful.

After a while, when you've become accustomed to the practise and enjoy it more, you can gradually increase from five minutes to ten minutes a day, maybe to twenty. Don't push yourself to extremes trying to achieve a top performance; it is, after all, a training in kindness! It's better to sit for fifteen minutes twice a day than an hour once a day. It's better to sit for fifteen minutes once a day than two hours straight once a week.

Of course, there's still a lot more to explain about meditation. There are many other techniques, all of which – in a different way – aim for the same goal: a kind, calm mind that realises its own nature. Later in this book you'll come across some more exercises that you can include in your daily practice. And in Appendix 1 there are suggestions for courses and books that can help you further. But there's no reason why you shouldn't start right now. Decide that you'll keep doing it for at least two weeks before you think about whether you want to go on. And start right now! You'll see how soon you begin to enjoy it.

16

Painful emotions: the door to your natural state

*Hell is not punishment,
it's training.*

Shunryu Suzuki, Zen master
(1904-1971)

You don't practise meditation in order to become a good meditator. You do it in order to develop kindness in your daily life, towards yourself and others, and to learn how to live from within your natural perfect state of being. It's therefore essential that the progress you make in your meditation practise is truly applied in your daily life. Meditation and your daily life must increasingly blend together. There are many different techniques that can also help you with this. One of them is the '1-minute meditation'. You can use it any time of day, as often as you like, whenever you have a spare moment; at the bus stop or in the toilet, or when you're going from one activity to the next. You just do the same thing as in the formal meditation practise: sit down (or remain standing) with a straight back, relaxed and alert, and bring attention to your breathing, while your mind is aware of itself for a moment. Let everything in your mind and around you just happen, without changing any aspect of it. Then after a minute, simply get on with your day-to-day concerns again. You'll see that after a while these brief moments of refuge will start to radiate a calming influence on the rest of your day.

Another helpful technique is the 'lightning-flash' exercise. You can also do this any time of day, whenever you think of it. Stop what you're doing for a moment, focus your mind on itself and ask yourself with kindness, 'How am I feeling right now?' Very briefly, focus the light of your attention on your body and feelings, without changing any aspect of them. Then immediately get back to what you were doing.

You'll notice that maybe you intend to do these exercises, but at first you almost never get around to them spontaneously. You simply forget, so you need a bit of a helping hand. You can put a few small reminders at various places in your house, such as a card with a question mark on it, a piece of ribbon tied in a bow round a door handle, a pebble on the kitchen-sink draining board. Whenever you see the reminder, ask yourself, 'How am I feeling right now?' And look with kindness at how you're feeling; for when you're not at home, you can tie the traditional knot in your handkerchief, or put a pebble in your trouser pocket, or write a question mark on your hand. For months I had a piece of string tied around my ring finger. Whenever you think about it, bring your mind back to itself, give yourself attention without judging, and without wanting to change anything. And then immediately get on with your daily life again.

These mini-exercises in applied meditation are at least as important as the formal meditation practise in your regular meditation place. Formal meditation practise can be compared to filling a thermos flask with kind, non-judgemental awareness. During the day you can use this for a cupful of kind awareness in the '1-minute meditations', and a quick sip in the 'lightning-flash' exercises. The formal practise increases the strength and clarity of your mind. But doing the quick informal exercises during the day increases the stability of the mind in any circumstance. And the combination of these forms of practice increasingly gives the mind the capacity to undertake the highest form of training on the spiritual path: the transformation of painful and distressing emotions into clarity and love.

But before you start on that most important training, it's best to prepare with the practise of loving kindness. This is a simple exercise in developing kind, non-judgemental observation, regardless of the object of that observation. Start by bringing your mind back home to itself, in the manner explained in the last chapter. After a few minutes of being attentively present with everything that's occurring in and around you, start on the real exercise. Try to evoke a feeling of loving kindness in yourself. All possible means are permitted. You can use memories of a loving person in your life, or a situation where you felt loved or treated kindly. You can use a photo or a few lines of text, or anything at all that can evoke a feeling of loving kindness in you, no matter how small that might be. Then start the visualisation.

Traditionally, this exercise involves the visualisation of an image of a Buddha or a spiritual master, as the embodiment of the highest spiritual love. But you can also use a different inspiring image, or simply visualise a source of clear, warm light. From that light source, allow love in the form of a warm, radiant light to flow into yourself. Try to really create a glimmer of a warm, loving feeling in yourself. Once you've achieved this to some extent, let go of the whole visualisation and focus your loving attention on yourself, on your body and your breathing. You see, we usually think we can only look lovingly at something that evokes love in us. But with this exercise you first use a loving object to evoke loving kindness in yourself, and then you transform those feelings into a loving way of looking. Looking at something that's loving then changes into looking lovingly. You then focus that loving look on yourself and your breathing. When the loving feeling starts to fade, you can go back to the first part of the exercise and evoke a little more loving kindness in yourself. Once you've done this, continue with looking lovingly at yourself and your breathing.

In order to train the stability of looking lovingly, after a while you can also choose a slightly more difficult object and, for instance, focus your loving look on someone you hardly know, or even someone you dislike. You'll be amazed at how this exercise changes your perception of annoying people and painful situations. And each time you lose this loving way of looking, go back to the start of the exercise and evoke another new store of loving kindness in yourself.

This becomes even more challenging if you try to look lovingly at yourself in a situation where you felt ashamed or guilty. Try to look with kindness – even if very briefly – at a painful memory of self-rejection. Or at someone who made you feel very rejected. And if you can't do that, then try to look at *that* with kindness. If you practise this for a while, you develop a kind and loving way of looking. But note carefully, looking in a kind and loving way doesn't necessarily mean that you must also have a kind or loving feeling. It mostly means that your way of looking becomes open and non-judgemental, sympathetic and accepting, regardless of what you feel at that moment. In this way, you can free yourself from the distress that constantly arises if your way of looking is determined by what you're looking at. Can you see that you usually think it's stupid if you feel stupid? That you usually look angrily at your own anger? That you strongly reject yourself when you feel rejected? That you immediately and automatically reject someone who rejects you? Time after time, our natural kind awareness is coloured by thoughts and emotions we're looking at. Time after time, we let our way of looking be determined by the object we're looking at. That isn't freedom, it's oppression. And you can learn to stop doing it by practising loving kindness. The more stable your loving and non-judgemental observation becomes, the more you'll be able to use your painful emotions as the door to your natural state of being. That's what the next exercise is about.

In Chapter 8 you read about how you create painful emotions by identifying with them, and make them worse by resisting them. The way this happened was first, there's a thought or circumstance – the so-called 'trigger' – that evokes a memory of a painful feeling from the past. The mind is immediately swept along by a stream of thoughts: it identifies with that memory and resists it. In a fraction of a second, what is initially a mental image of a painful emotion from the past changes into real pain in the present. We don't want that pain, so our resistance grows. This in turn increases the pain, and the circle of samsara is complete. In addition, we very often take action on the basis of this painful vicious circle, thus creating new circumstances that in turn act as the trigger for more misery. If you reject or manipulate other people, they are more likely to also reject or manipulate you. In short, this is how we constantly create new pain out of old pain. With meditation you train the mind in the opposite direction. In this, you go through a number of different stages.

The first stage begins when you become aware that you've ended up in a painful emotion (and therefore stop being merged with it), and also don't try to immediately get rid of it (and therefore don't immediately start to dissociate). Instead, you try to stay attentively present with yourself, without acting on the basis of that emotion but with an attitude of kindness towards yourself and your painful emotion. In short, you *allow* yourself to feel bad about yourself, without attaching self-rejecting conclusions to it. This doesn't instantly make the feeling less painful, but what you achieve at this stage is that you don't create new misery as a reaction to the present misery. And the misery doesn't last as long, because you offer less resistance to it. You learn to trust the transient nature of emotions: after all, have you ever found that the same emotion lasts for more than a day, or even an hour? The less resistance you offer to an emotion, the sooner it dissolves and makes way for the next, and then the next. In fact, it's impossible for a painful emotion to spontaneously exist – if you don't get agitated about it – for more than a few minutes. You can compare this to breaking wind: in a small room the smell lingers for a long time, but on top of a mountain it disperses immediately. By resisting a negative emotion, you make your mind small and confined; all the space is consumed by that emotion. But if your mind is spacious and open, the negative emotions disperse immediately.

In the second stage of the training you use the painful feeling as the object of your meditation. You very gently bring your attention to the physical aspect of the emotion, while you also remain present in a spacious and open way, and your mind is conscious of itself. You'll notice that your mind keeps trying to wander off to the story that caused this misery: 'he mustn't leave me, she should be honest, this shouldn't have happened'. You're actually trying to stop the pain with your thinking. You're searching frantically for the redeeming thought, the most apposite reproach of the other person, the most justified denial of your own responsibility, the smartest way to get out of the painful situation. But the more you think, the more real the story becomes, and the more painful the feeling. Yet you'll automatically keep running away from your pain and circling around the story. It doesn't matter: each time you notice that you're doing it, simply stop without judging and bring your attention back to the physical aspect (some people call this the 'energetic' aspect) of your painful emotion. But don't try not to think about the story in your head, because that's also a way of fighting it. Just keep bringing your attention back to your body, to the place where your painful feeling is located, such as your throat, chest or stomach. In this stage it can be beneficial to use a kind of mantra that reminds you of your training. 'It doesn't matter, it's OK, just let it be' helps to release resistance to the pain, for example. 'I'm allowed to feel this, I am not my feeling' helps you to stop judging yourself. Repeat these phrases from time to time in your head or out loud, to help you keep your attention with the feeling itself.

At the beginning you mustn't do this exercise for too long, because it will soon become contrived. Look at your painful emotion for a few minutes at a time, and then do something else. Allow yourself to use non-destructive forms of escape: phone a good friend, clean your house, read an engrossing book, make yourself a nice cup of tea. Any time your misery feels too painful, sit in your meditation position for a few minutes, looking directly at the physical sensation of your negative emotion.

At this stage you'll notice that you will become less afraid of your negative feelings. After they've been evoked by a thought, a person, or a situation, you'll become quicker at recognising them as negative emotions, and not run away from them so much. As a result, they'll also become less distressing and won't last nearly as long. You won't take the story that caused the distress so seriously. If you notice that you still keep getting stuck in your victim role, and hold other people responsible for your distress or reject yourself, then it's time to lay your story to rest and let go of being right. This doesn't mean that you're wrong, but that you think it's more important to be happy than to be right. A cognitive therapy or training can help you with this.

In the third stage of this training you not only use your painful emotion, but also your resistance to it as the object of meditation. You've obviously worked on letting go of your resistance at the first two stages, and this has been of great benefit to you: the distress is reducing and does not last as long. Yet there's still resistance to the emotion, because all your training is focused on stopping the misery. You still want to get rid of it, and meditation is your new method. But this approach only works to a certain extent. In this third stage you try to find the most subtle form of resistance to the painful emotion. Sit in the meditation position and again start by taking the physical aspect of your painful emotion as the object of your attention. Then try to see and feel that within your body there's also a subtle kind of tensing-up around the painful emotion, a kind of 'pushing away' feeling. Try to localise that tensing-up sensation and bring it into your awareness. Don't do anything about it, just look at it without judgement while your mind is conscious of this exercise. In this way, the subtle tension will also gradually decrease.

Sometimes, as a temporary aid, you can try to intensify the pain of the emotion. Try to deliberately feel even more worthless, more lonely, more angry than you already do. It isn't important whether you succeed or not: in the meantime your subtle resistance to the pain loses a little of its strength. You can also think of painful emotions as a door to your natural state of being. Look at your pain with interest, with respect and devotion, as if it were a precious treasure. Remember the example of the rope that in the twilight was mistaken for a snake. If you want to lose your fear of the snake, you have to look at it carefully, until you see that it's actually a piece of rope. In the same way, your painful emotions are in reality not painful emotions, but a pure manifestation of your natural state of being. There's only one way to find out whether this is just a nice little spiritual story, or whether it's really true: look for yourself, and look, and keep on looking. Look without judgement. Look with kind, non-judgemental awareness. Look at the pain. And look at your most subtle resistance to the pain.

And then one day it happens: when *all* your resistance and tension dissolves for a moment, when you even forget to hope for an enlightenment experience, then suddenly the miracle happens; while you're looking at it, the pain suddenly turns out not to be pain at all, but a little cloud of energy, so pure and clean and clear! Amazed and filled with happiness, you see it happen: there is no pain, there never *was* pain, it was always the mind that judged and ran away. It was always the mind that was mistaken, and became tensed-up around that mistake. It was the mind itself that suffered pain because it thought it saw pain, just as it had been taught since early childhood to see pain where in reality there is only pure, clean, enlightened energy. An incredible joy flows through you, and a deep feeling of love: everyone must discover this!

When you have this experience, however, it doesn't mean you're enlightened; but it *does* mean you no longer have any doubt about your natural state, and the possibility of realising it. Your old tendency to run away from your painful feelings hasn't immediately worn off either. The first trap into which you'll undoubtedly fall the next time you feel a painful emotion is to try – by looking at it attentively – to repeat that fantastic experience. Time after time, you must unlearn that reflex of running away, and instead truly surrender to your pain. But of course you'll become better and faster at that when you've already experienced that it really works. At first you'll often still spend a couple of hours wrestling with yourself before you suddenly again find that opening in which all tensing-up dissolves and the pain transforms into pure energy. But your progress will be unmistakable: each time you'll see through the illusion of suffering more quickly. Eventually, it will be the pain itself that reminds you of your natural state, so that the arising and dissolving of the pain take place almost simultaneously. Then pain loses all negative meaning; each time, it brings you directly into contact with your natural state, and with the enlightened energy that springs from that: love and clarity.

This is why practising meditation, and especially meditation with your painful emotions, heralds the end of your dependence on other people's love and approval. This meditation enables your hardened, ego-protecting patterns to gradually dissolve. As a result, you become *really* independent. I should point out, however, that this doesn't mean you have to stay sitting in splendid isolation and supreme ecstasy on some mountain top: your 'need consciousness' changes into an 'abundance consciousness', so you can do nothing other than share your happiness and your love with others, in the way that's most appropriate for you. Whatever you do, it will contribute to the happiness of yourself and others. Your work will bring you greater joy, and if it doesn't, you'll start to do different work that suits you better. Your relationship will become more loving, and if it doesn't, you'll start to live alone or find another relationship. Some friendships will become more intense, while other friends will disappear from your life; new special encounters will take place. Your life will flow because you're *whole*, you're open and loving, as you always already were but never experienced before. *This*, and being able to help others experience the same thing, is the greatest gift you give yourself with the practise of meditation.

17

Integration instead of dissociation

*There are no obstacles on the spiritual path,
obstacles are the path.*

Buddhist saying

There are two kinds of blocks to our development: merging with a safe ego pattern and dissociation from an unsafe one. We saw in Chapter 7 that merging is a form of attachment to what protects us from rejection, while dissociation is a form of self-rejection. Merging ends because you become conscious of a pattern. Immediately after this, there's a strong tendency to dissociate, because the new 'self-consciousness' immediately overshoots into self-rejection: the just-discovered ego pattern must be eliminated! We think that development can only happen by fighting and eradicating the 'lower' automatic responses, such as fears, compulsions, aversions, and addictions. However, those suppressed automatic responses start to live their own life underground, re-emerge at unexpected moments, and act as permanent ballast. Therefore something that was aimed at development in fact becomes a hindrance. The reason is that we don't recognise the unwanted aspects of our identity as the blocked or mutilated version of natural qualities. Thus arrogance, for example, is the ego version of intelligence, macho toughness is the distorted version of strength, and the 'nice guy' syndrome is the twisted version of pure kindness. It's fear of rejection and self-rejection that turns those natural qualities into a distorted 'ego variant', with which we are then merged for some time.

After a while, there arises – spontaneously or through training or therapy – an awareness of this merging and its disadvantages for our development. And then we usually make the crucial mistake: we reject the aspect of our self-image with which we were initially merged as negative, worthless, bad, stupid, not good enough, or whatever our negative belief might be. And we try to dissociate from it. If we succeed in this, the dissociated part then goes underground, from where it undermines our sense of self-esteem. In the longer term, it can cause all kinds of disturbing symptoms at the emotional and physical level. If we fail or only partially succeed in dissociating, then we stay embroiled in a constant fight against the unwanted characteristic, and hence against ourselves.

This tendency to dissociate can be seen at all levels of our functioning: it makes us maintain an artificial image and self-image, and prefer to amputate a part of ourselves than miss out on other people's love and approval. It makes us try to escape from our painful emotions, and thus constantly create new misery. It makes us completely powerless against our own stream of thoughts, going around and around in all kinds of distressing stories about reality, the past, or the future. In short: dissociation is the engine behind mental and emotional misery. And the driver of that engine is our inner judge or critic, also known as the superego.

In Chapter 3 the inner critic was compared to a policeman or judge who enforces the rules in the second layer of our identity. Those are the rules that we have to obey in order to get the love and approval that protect us from our negative belief. Now that we've more or less completed the survey of all the counterproductive misunderstandings in our self-image, we can see that this inner judge is actually what causes almost all the misery in our life. Or in other words: it's the personification of all the misunderstandings that together constitute our self-image. We know our inner judge as an inner voice that advises us to do certain things and not to do other things, by pointing out the pros and cons in relation to other people's love and approval. 'If you do this, you'll get lots of praise. If you do that, you could seriously lose respect.' But when you only do something in order to get people's praise, or don't do something only out of fear of rejection, your inner judge is instantly ready to attack with self-rejection: you're such a creep or attention-seeker, in the first case; such a wimp or weakling, in the second case. Your relationship with your inner judge is a no-win situation: whether you obey it or fight it, you always lose. That's because your inner judge is actually the internalised version of the voice of your parents when you were young. Each time you hear the voice of the inner judge, you feel as small and powerless as you did when you were a child. If you do what the voice says, you lose your autonomy; if you don't, then you're stupid, weak, or bad. There's only one way to get out of this situation, and that is to 'de-authorise' the entire inner judge. In order to do that, you must first see clearly how you 'authorise' it, how you unconsciously give it power, time after time. Three styles can be distinguished in this:

1 *Self-destruction*
You rebel against the inner judge. This happens, for instance, when it draws our attention to unhealthy or destructive behaviour. If we listen to it, we must keep ourselves very strictly under control: no alcohol, no over-eating, no smoking, no sweets, and so on. We can keep this up for a while, but we often get so utterly sick and tired of that control freak or anxious inner voice that we rebel: 'I don't give a damn whether it's unhealthy, or stupid, or bad, I'm going to do it anyway!' And of course, once the binge is over, the inner judge will be ready and waiting to reproach you that yes, indeed, you're stupid, weak, or bad.

2 *Self-justification*
You engage in discussion with the inner judge. For hours on end, we can come up with arguments in our head about why the criticism isn't true, and that really we *are* doing the right thing, that it wasn't selfish at all, that there were good reasons for this behaviour and that

the inner judge is being very unfair. But all that time, we actually feel rejected and never reach the point where we're right.

3 Self-pity

You give in to the inner judge. You feel so overwhelmed by the criticism that you can only collapse into self-reproach. It's true, the inner judge is right, you're a weakling, a worthless good-for-nothing, and you'll never achieve anything.

So you can see that rebelling (self-destruction), negotiating (self-justification), and giving in (self-pity) all have the same effect: you lose your autonomy and give the power to the inner judge. The reason is that, in all cases, you acknowledge in advance that the inner judge has the right to criticise you. There's never any doubt about its position of power, so we can only direct our resistance against the contents of the criticism. But in doing this, we only strengthen its position of power. It's just the same as with your parents when you were young: whether you agreed with them or resisted them, in the end you were always the weaker one, the one who had to submit to them. You could only be independent after you'd left the parental home. Even after that, many people remain afraid of their parents for a very long time. This is because our parents are the outer version of our inner judge, and until we've removed the latter from its position of authority, we haven't got things straightened out with the former. For several decades after I'd left home, my father could still provoke my anger and resistance, simply through the schoolmasterly tone in which he laid claim to being right. It was only after I'd fired my inner judge, and was more or less in harmony with myself (and with the schoolmaster in me), that I could be in his presence without getting annoyed by his behaviour. Eventually, during the last years of his life, I was even able to laugh with him and at him, and found it endearing when yet again he started to explain to me how I should be feeling.

As long as you continue to react to the contents of your inner judge's criticism, you surrender your autonomy and increase its influence.

To release your inner judge, you must make the decision that you're never going to abandon yourself again. Rather than engaging with the contents of its criticism, you completely deprive it of the right to criticise you at all.

In fact, this means that you'll never consciously reject yourself again. And that isn't so easy; sometimes you won't succeed, so you have to start by no longer rejecting yourself for the fact that you occasionally reject yourself. The best way to develop this non-rejecting consciousness is – you've already guessed – meditation. Basically, the mind that is conscious of itself, the self-aware awareness, is always free from rejection and self-rejection. Development of that clear, non-judgemental awareness is the ultimate way to put an end to your self-rejection. In addition, there are also practical psychological methods to free yourself from the inner judge, but these fall outside the scope of this book (see Appendix 1).

The last chapter was about looking at your painful emotions and at the tensing-up reaction to the pain, which increases and maintains them. That tensing-up is, in the most extreme instance, self-rejection. Rejection of both your painful emotion and yourself creates the vicious circle in which you push away the pain, but in doing so actually increase and maintain it. The problem isn't your anger, but your rejection of the anger and of yourself if you feel angry; this causes you to vent your anger on the person or situation that evoked it. And that, in turn, creates new misery. The problem isn't your craving (for sex, drugs, food or sweets, for instance), but your rejection of that craving and of yourself as the 'craver'; this makes you want to eliminate your craving, and to do this you must satisfy it. The problem isn't your loneliness, but your rejection of it and of yourself if you're lonely. Loneliness is actually nothing other than being stuck with someone you don't like, namely yourself. As a result, you feel compelled to seek companionship, distraction or some form of sedation, and if that doesn't work or has worn off, you feel even more lonely.

Every ego pattern is in fact an automatic response aimed at protecting yourself against rejection, and obtaining love and approval. Each time you become conscious of one of these patterns, you have the tendency to dissociate from it. But it's absolutely not the ego pattern itself that causes the problem, but the self-rejection which it conceals, and which emerges at the conscious meta-level as a rejection of the whole pattern. It's the rejection of the self-rejection that sustains the self-rejecting self-image. And you can learn to stop doing that!

Instead of dissociating, you can learn to integrate the ego pattern concerned. This means that you learn to look at it without self-rejection. When you do this, the self-rejection that was inherent in the ego pattern will also disappear. And that pattern will then gradually change into the original natural quality that was always its core. Thus you'll see that arrogance, for example, when you no longer reject it but embrace it with your non-judgemental awareness, will gradually blossom as pure intelligence or clarity. Perhaps you discover that you're a helpaholic. Stop rejecting yourself about it, embrace it and let your natural altruism break free. Are you ashamed that you manipulate other people in order to get attention? Stop being ashamed, embrace your attention-seeking and let your natural creativity and artistry unfold from it. Are you a conflict-avoider, a 'nice guy', and do you try to fight that tendency and become assertive? Stop doing that, embrace your 'nice guy' pattern and allow your natural kindness to develop. Are you ashamed of your addictive behaviour? Don't be ashamed, embrace your addiction and let your natural longing for happiness and harmony emerge from it. If you do this, there's no doubt that very soon you'll reach the point where you cease your addiction and self-destruction. Are you a perfectionist and always very tough on yourself? Embrace it with non-judgemental awareness, and the entire pattern will lose its oppression and reveal its natural form: integrity and longing for completeness.

Have you done the mirror test that I described at the end of Chapter 2? (No? Then do it now, before you read the explanation that follows here!) I also mentioned this test in my previous books, and have received many responses from readers who have done it. What most people experience during the mirror test is NOTHING. But then in a very special way you briefly experience the absence of any negative feeling about yourself. There's an awareness that the sentences spoken about your negative belief, such as 'I am weak' or 'I am worthless', bear absolutely no relation to the person who's speaking them, that in fact they bear absolutely no relation to anything. By saying your negative belief out loud, you're actually doing the opposite of what your identity normally makes you do: to conceal it. Precisely by trying to conceal it, you give it a kind of reality value, and during the mirror test it very briefly loses this. This creates a moment of purely being present. Some people have said that after this they felt sad or emotional. Feeling sad is sometimes the result of seeing how much suffering this identity construction has already caused for other people and yourself. Feeling emotional comes from the sense of pureness and closeness. Some people just laughed out loud, or simply stood looking at themselves with a big, liberating grin.

On the other hand, there's a small chance that the negative belief will actually be evoked during the mirror test. In that case, saying it out loud makes you suddenly experience feelings of worthlessness, which is really very fortunate! After all, because you've now evoked those negative feelings yourself, you have an exceptional opportunity to remain present with them, instead of lapsing into the standard reaction of condemning them and covering them up again as soon as possible. Within this non-judgemental awareness, the negative feelings will quite quickly subside, after which you'll experience a sense of independence and strength.

You see, in reality there's nothing to reject. But because we're not conscious of this perfection, self-rejection arises, and that in turn gives rise to our ego patterns. And the only thing that sustains them is self-rejection. You don't need to improve anything at all about yourself in order to be a good and worthwhile human being. It's enough to simply stop believing that you aren't good and worthwhile yet. Whatever it is that you see as wrong about yourself, embrace it with non-judgemental awareness. Don't try to love yourself if that isn't what you feel: it's enough to just look without judgement. Sympathetically. Kindly. Generously. And with the insight and confidence that the goodness that is within you will emerge naturally, provided you don't interfere too much. It's only by making that unconditional choice in favour of yourself, by developing that kind, non-judgemental way of looking at yourself, other people, and the world, that your natural state of being will increasingly manifest itself in your life and in everything you do.

'Yes, but,' you might think, 'pretending that everything is fine and hunky-dory, isn't that just a denial of all the misery in the world?' But no: the intention isn't that you close your eyes to all the misery in the world, just that you let go of your condemnation of it. Because that condemnation is completely pointless and even counterproductive; it contributes nothing to the well-being of yourself and of the world. Precisely that tendency to condemn, which sustains all kinds of misery in yourself, also makes you feel powerless in relation to the misery in the world. But if you stop condemning, and simply let the world be as it is, right now, then your pity and powerless frustration will change into compassion and effortless action for the well-being of yourself and everyone else. If it actually helped, condemnation would perhaps be alright. But it doesn't help at all, not in any way whatsoever. Condemnation and self-rejection really only create misery for yourself and the world. So isn't it time to break out of that oppressive vicious circle in yourself, and to start embracing everything in and around yourself in non-judgemental awareness? The advantages of this are really so much greater than you can now imagine. There's simply no limit to the happiness that's set free when you realise your natural state of being.

18

The natural state of being: belief or reality?

*Great doubt, great enlightenment;
small doubt, small enlightenment;
no doubt, no enlightenment.*

Zen saying

In this book there have been many references to a natural state of being, a perfect nature, which we are all supposed to have. As yet, however, the arguments for this have only been indirect: they've shown that our failure to see a perfect nature, plus our belief in an imperfect and needy nature, is the cause of suffering. So are there also logical arguments that can directly prove the existence of a perfect nature? No, there aren't – no more than the existence of an imperfect nature can be proved with logical arguments. Some people will point at all the misery in the world as an argument in favour of the proposition that human beings have a basic inclination towards evil. Others look at the signs of goodness and altruism, and presume that our nature is fundamentally good. Most people take a view somewhere in the middle, and see every human being as the result of a struggle between their good and bad qualities or inclinations. Our ordinary everyday observation doesn't give a logical answer that decides this debate.

But on a contemplative level, you'll see that people with many 'bad' qualities don't seem to be very happy. The murderer, the dictator, the rapist: they don't make a particularly happy and harmonious impression. Also on a smaller scale, it's clear that people who have an addiction, or tell a lot of lies, who manipulate, steal, or in other ways harm themselves or others, don't find much peace and inner serenity in this in the longer term. Yet if causing harm were our deepest nature, then that should make us feel most peaceful and harmonious. If lying and cheating were our deepest nature, then that should bring us more – rather than less – inner peace and harmony. If aggression were our deepest nature, then we should be happiest in times of war and violence. So the fact that people sometimes lie and cheat, or are aggressive and violent, doesn't stem from their deepest nature, even if it gives them a short-lived form of happiness. We sometimes think that lying and cheating will make us happier, we sometimes use violence as a solution to a problem, we sometimes turn to destructive means to escape from misery and strive for happiness. But the happiness produced by these negative actions is actually nothing other than a temporary reduction of the distress that made us engage in them. At the same time, it's clear that in the longer term these negative actions don't enduringly give more happiness, but in fact create more distress.

When you look at people's behaviour in this way, at their positive and negative actions, and the happiness or distress resulting from them, then it suddenly becomes quite obvious that our deepest nature is pure goodness. This immediately puts an end to all religious and moral value systems. Good and bad don't exist as such. Actions are positive if they result in more happiness (for yourself and others), and negative if they result in more misery. Or in other words: an action is positive if it's in harmony with our deepest nature, and negative if it conflicts with it.

But this is perhaps just a fine-sounding argument to prove that a perfect nature exists, so the only way to be really 100% certain is to realise that nature *yourself*. The method for achieving this realisation is called the spiritual path and, contrary to the common conception, this method is actually very 'scientific'. After all, in science too, a theory is first formulated to explain (an aspect of) reality. Then experiments are conducted to see whether this theory is correct. The results determine whether the theory is (provisionally) accepted or rejected. It's exactly the same procedure on the spiritual path: first the basic hypothesis is posited that all human beings have a perfect nature. Then an experiment is proposed: allow the mind to turn inward and look at its own nature. Resources are provided: various meditation techniques, from beginner's level to highly advanced, are available to the 'researcher'. There are also 'scientific' publications: writings in which, through the centuries, advanced practitioners, teachers and sages report their research, confirm the hypothesis and give further instructions for those who wish to apply this research themselves. In short, the spiritual path is identical to science in many ways: the spiritual method is rational (in line with logic and reasoning) and functional (the results are decisive). The Buddha himself said that his teachings weren't meant to be simply accepted and believed, but to be applied for oneself. He compared his spiritual teachings to a finger pointing at the moon. Only a fool would think that the finger is more important than what it's pointing at. Buddhism regards itself as a means that intends to make itself redundant, like a raft that can take you across a river. Once you've realised that perfect nature yourself, once you're on the other side of the river, you no longer need the raft and can let go of all spiritual 'research methods'.

The spiritual path is therefore the training that brings realisation of your perfect natural state of being. And at first sight that appears to contain a contradiction, because surely you can't learn a natural state? Wouldn't it then be an artificial, created state? And yes, that's right, you can't learn your natural state, you can only learn to stop denying and covering it. The natural state is already there, but we're usually not conscious of it. Instead of *being* our open and non-judgemental mind, and *experiencing* our thoughts and feelings from there, we constantly let ourselves be carried along by those thoughts and feelings, and take them very personally. We've completely identified ourselves with the contents of our mind, and are totally alienated from the mind itself, the kind, non-judgemental observer that's conscious of its own all-encompassing, abundant warmth and clarity, that needs nothing and gives effortlessly, and allows everyone to share in its abundance. Without realisation of that nature of the mind, we're tossed around on the wild waves of our thoughts and emotions. The nature of the mind is like the water, it permeates all our thoughts and emotions. As soon as we realise that we're the water, and not the individual pleasurable and painful waves, we are free.

Another frequently used example is that our observing mind is tied onto the horse of our thoughts and emotions. That horse reacts wildly and fearfully to all kinds of stimuli: it runs erratically, rearing and prancing, through the meadow of our life. This makes us just as fearful as the horse, and we try to calm it down by hitting and kicking it (self-rejection). You understand that this has a counterproductive effect. So our mind always remains as wild as an uncontrollable horse, and we ourselves remain fearful and dependent.

The spiritual path teaches you to stop hitting the horse, and instead to quieten it with kindness. You don't have to get it completely under control. If it becomes just a bit less wild and more inclined to co-operate with the rider, then you're free to occasionally dismount. You're no longer the victim of your own mind, but rather its observer; the rider who can use it or let go of it, whenever you want.

If you don't have any meditation experience yet, and you'd like to test the validity of this example, then you should spend five minutes – alone and without distraction – simply looking at your own mind and trying to keep your attention on one thing, such as a flower or your own breathing. When someone's never done this before, it can be quite frustrating and disconcerting to notice that your mind hardly ever stops, even for a moment. And that's when things are quiet, with no strong emotions in your body. Especially during difficult and distressing periods in your life, your own mind can drive you absolutely crazy, and for some people this literally happens. Depression and neuroses are also the consequence of a mind that's totally entangled and trapped in the battle against its own thoughts. It's not surprising that 'mindfulness training' is becoming so popular in mental health care, because the results are remarkably good. And this only involves quietening the mind, which doesn't in itself lead to spiritual realisation: for this, not only must the horse become calmer, but you must also discover that you are the rider who can use it or dismount at will. The mind must not only be quietened, but must also find and develop its own nature. You must learn to see through the many obscuring layers of patterns of thinking, feeling and behaving in order to be really free from your own thoughts and emotions. Again, this doesn't mean you no longer have thoughts and emotions, or only have pleasant ones. It means you no longer *are* your thoughts and emotions, and can recognise them as a game of the mind. It's a freedom beyond hope and fear, beyond pleasure and pain, beyond gain or loss, beyond being loved or rejected, beyond being appreciated or ignored. It is clear happiness and pure love.

When you start meditating, for example for five minutes a day, you'll very soon notice a quietening effect. This encourages you to meditate more, and to read inspiring spiritual 'research reports'. You develop a fascination with all available knowledge about the perfect nature of our mind. You read reports of other practitioners, and start to try new techniques that take you to deeper layers of your own mind. You have numerous moments of joy about new discoveries. You increasingly see that your interaction with other people also changes, you become kinder, less defensive, more open, and you live more from a calm, peaceful place deep within yourself.

Then one day you'll have your first direct experience of your perfect nature, an experience filled with amazing joy! A deep certainty develops within you, your meditation practise becomes more inspiring, you are more able to experience negative feelings without identifying with them, so your need to escape into distraction steadily declines. Your life becomes more simple, your relationships more profound and fulfilling. Those brief glimpses of your perfect nature become more frequent during your meditation practise, until you eventually succeed in evoking them yourself. Your everyday life gradually becomes lighter, and is increasingly filled with a quiet, permanent joy and a sparkling sense of humour. While this doesn't mean that you're now enlightened in the ultimate sense of the word, this actually starts to become less important. Because simply being happy and sharing that happiness with others is wonderful enough in itself.

So, the spiritual path is ultimately about realising your perfect natural state of being, which Buddhists also refer to as the 'nature of the mind', or 'Buddha nature'. Many books have been written about the methods for realising this nature, but if you're expecting to find a simple description of what this nature actually is, you'll be disappointed. That's because it can't be directly described. After all, descriptions are words, sentences, thoughts, and the nature of the mind is also the nature of those words, sentences and thoughts. The nature of the mind is the knowing quality that enables us – whenever we see, hear, think or feel something – to also *know* that we're seeing, hearing, thinking or feeling it. But that knowing quality, which is conscious of observations and thoughts, is not itself a thing or an identifiable phenomenon; if you look at it directly, there's never 'something' to see. The nature of the mind has that knowing quality without actually being an entity itself. All phenomena, thoughts, and feelings are experiences in that knowing 'non-entity' of the nature of the mind. All experiences, despairs, and delights of samsara are experiences in the nature of the mind. A common metaphor used to explain this is the movie projector. On the screen are the experiences in which we're usually entangled, and which cause the temporary happiness and misery of samsara. We're so absorbed by those phenomena that we lose ourselves in the illusion that the movie is reality. We forget that it's an illusion, created by 'the nature' of the cinema: the light from the projector. That light is what gives all the images their apparently real form, but the light itself doesn't play a part in the movie. As long as we lose ourselves in the projections, we're tied to the suffering of samsara. But the more we realise that we're the light source, the open and aware quality of the mind, the less we get entangled in the projections, and the more we become free from the suffering. That shift from your identification with the projections to that which is doing the projecting, from your restrictive identity to the liberating nature of everything, that is what you learn on the spiritual path. That path changes all painful problems into steps on the way to realisation. It gives meaning to what otherwise appears so senseless, namely the suffering, and causes this to gradually diminish and ultimately disappear out of your life. Isn't that fantastic?

19

The spiritual love relationship

Love one another, but make not a bond of love:
Let it rather be a moving sea between the shores of your souls.
Give one another of your bread, but eat not from the same loaf.
Sing and dance together and be joyous, but let each of you be alone,
And stand together yet not too near together:
As the oak tree and the cypress grow not in each other's shadow.

Khalil Gibran, Lebanese poet
(1883-1931) from: The Prophet

It's not your job to understand me.
That's my job.

Byron Katie

When you've let go of relationship thinking, this doesn't mean you'll never be able to have a love relationship again. The only thing that changes is that the relationship is no longer the most important goal in your life, but a means to help you on the spiritual path. This might seem to devalue the highest form of happiness that is often associated with the love relationship. 'A relationship as a means to help you on the path' doesn't sound very romantic, rather as if love changes into working hard for spiritual progress. Nothing could be further from the truth! A spiritual love relationship actually offers everything you were striving for with an ordinary love relationship but were never – and will never be – able to achieve, because that method itself is counterproductive. In the spiritual relationship, the love is no longer suffocated by fear and the need for safety, so it just keeps growing and flowering! As you no longer primarily need the other person for your security and self-esteem (because you find those in yourself) it becomes increasingly effortless to give unconditional love, and you quite naturally receive more love in return. In fact, over time the distinction between giving and receiving love disappears, and the relationship becomes a total and voluntary merging of two independent and complete human beings in one single experience of love. This is therefore a kind of reversed image of the merging of two fearful half-people in one single symbiotic oppression, as often occurs in a traditional love relationship. Here too we see that in our perfect nature the capacity for unconditionally loving and merging was always already present, but that in many relationships this quality is mutilated by fear and self-rejection, so that it becomes a restrictive and painful shadow of itself. Love is mutilated to become security, connectedness is twisted into clinging, effortless giving disappears behind making efforts to receive. The idea that the spiritual path would rob you of your (chance of) love-related happiness is actually very much like the fear of addicts who are thinking of stopping: although the addiction causes a downward spiral of misery in their life, they're still afraid that their life will be grey and dull and devoid of happiness after they stop. In the same way, letting go of relationship thinking creates the fear that your life will be lonely and loveless. But if you embrace this fear and recognise it as a mistake, this will in fact be the start of a path that's more filled with love and fulfilment than you ever could have dreamed!

And of course you can still let go of relationship thinking if you aren't currently in a relationship. Because choosing to follow a spiritual path also includes changing your attitude to a future love relationship: you stop chasing it, and learn to instantly use feelings of deprivation as the object of your practice. The more you can embrace those deep feelings of missing a partner yourself with non-judgemental awareness, the less dependent on other people's love and approval you become, and the more your 'need consciousness' changes into an 'abundance consciousness'. Then, if an opportunity for a new relationship presents itself, you're operating from a position of spiritual strength, and from the outset can allow your new relationship to blossom as never before. But a relationship is never really a necessity: happiness is in essence already fully present in yourself, and you can also share your happiness and love with others without having a relationship. So if you're not in a relationship at the moment, and you want to get started on a spiritual path, you already have one less obstacle than someone who *is* in a relationship. Because even though a relationship can be used as a means to help you on the path, it can also be a considerable hindrance to spiritual development, especially for a beginner.

Converting an existing traditional relationship into a spiritual one is certainly a challenge. After all, the relationship began when you were still controlled by your 'need consciousness', and therefore contains all kinds of overt and covert protection mechanisms, developed to guard you against rejection and self-rejection. Merely discussing the possibility of giving priority to the spiritual development of each individual, instead of the relationship, can result in deep fears. However, as soon as you see that those fears are actually a symptom of your inability to take care of yourself, they can also serve as a stimulus to go on with this spiritual project. Let's take a look at how you can set about converting your relationship into a spiritual relationship in practice. First we'll examine a stable relationship in which both partners have spiritual aspirations. Next we'll look at a relationship in crisis, and then finally at a stable relationship in which one of the partners feels no need for spirituality.

If you've both become inspired by a form of spirituality, the best way to start is by talking to each other a lot, and finding out how you can support each other on the spiritual path. You can look together at situations in which you evoke negative feelings in each other, and consider how each of you can take responsibility yourself for those feelings. For an example of this, we can have another look at Brett and Gina.

Gina has beautiful, long black hair (one of the reasons Brett fell in love with her), but every time she takes a shower, a few stray hairs are left behind in the drain cover. Brett gets really irritated by this, thinking that everyone should clear up after themselves. Sometimes he grumbles and removes Gina's hairs from the drain cover himself, other times he asks her to clean out those hairs before he takes a shower. Gina thinks his reaction is excessive and 'making an issue of it: I simply forgot about the hairs, very sorry'. This makes Brett feel that his perfectly justified complaint has been misunderstood. Both of them experience anger and frustration.

I'm deliberately choosing a very trivial problem, because you can clearly see that in this both parties need the other in order to get rid of their unpleasant feeling, instead of resolving it for themselves. Brett wants acknowledgement of his standpoint that everyone should clear up after themselves, and feels frustrated because he doesn't receive it. Gina doesn't give this acknowledgement because she first wants *him* to acknowledge that she simply forgets to clean out the hairs, and therefore isn't intentionally doing anything wrong. In a traditional relationship, this problem can't be resolved without at least one of the parties having to settle for frustration.

From a spiritual perspective, there isn't a problem here, but rather an opening for spiritual growth. Brett could start by recognising his frustration as an old feeling from his childhood, when he was often blamed for things that his younger sister had done. He would then be able to embrace with non-judgemental awareness this feeling of taking the blame for other people's misdeeds, and being misunderstood when he objects to this. This means he no longer needs Gina's acknowledgement: he is now the one who acknowledges his feeling of being misunderstood. 'Need consciousness' thus changes into 'abundance consciousness', and with love he now removes Gina's hairs from the drain cover, or leaves them there, as long as the water can still drain away.

Gina, for her part, could take responsibility herself for her feeling of rejection after being reproached by Brett. Her rejection of Brett's 'making an issue of it' is a reaction to her own painful feeling that she's done something wrong. In her family when she was young, making mistakes wasn't tolerated and was severely rejected. As soon as she recognises this feeling as an old feeling that's only being 'touched' by Brett, she can take responsibility for it herself and embrace it with non-judgemental awareness. This allows it to dissolve, she no longer feels dependent on Brett's acknowledgement, and can now react by cleaning the drain cover herself, or by pleasantly asking Brett to do it for her.

In this way, everything that in a traditional relationship creates tension and frustration can be used for transformation from 'need consciousness' into 'abundance consciousness', from dependence and needing approval into independence and giving love. 'She doesn't understand me, he blames me, she shouldn't do it that way, he should stop doing that, she doesn't appreciate me, he doesn't communicate, she doesn't take me as I am, he hurts me, she shouldn't nag so much, he shouldn't be so reserved, she must respect my boundaries, he must start to express his feelings', all the 'justified' reproaches of this kind would melt away like snow in the springtime sun. Misunderstanding, frustration, reproach, anger, and powerlessness would be recognised as *feelings* of misunderstanding, frustration, reproach, anger, and powerlessness. This enables you to feel them without identifying with them, and embrace them with non-judgemental awareness, whereupon they transform into autonomy and love.

An excellent resource if you're working with your partner on a more spiritual relationship is the 'turn-taking talk'. You sit facing each other, then one of you starts by talking about her experiences, her problems, what she finds hard to accept, and so on. The other is not permitted to respond, and at most may indicate that he understands, or ask a simple question for clarification. This goes on for a pre-determined period of time, such as five minutes, using a kitchen timer as an impartial observer. Then both of you should sit in silence for a short time, such as two minutes, giving attention to your breathing, or using another meditation technique that you enjoy. Then it's the other person's turn: after setting the kitchen timer for another five minutes, he can say whatever he thinks is important. When he's done this, you both sit in silence for a short time, and then the session ends. You can tell each other how you felt about the exercise, but try not to immediately start discussing what was actually said during the exercise. Even if you're left with a frightened or angry feeling, resolve it for yourself first, by meditating, or going for a walk, or anything else that works for you. If necessary, you can repeat the exercise a few hours later.

If you do this exercise quite often, you'll notice that you gradually start to speak more about your own experience, and feel less need to change your partner. 'You were an absolute pain this morning in the bathroom, whinging on about those hairs in the shower drain again' changes into 'I felt very rejected and guilty this morning, when you started on about those hairs in the shower drain'. And as the listening party, you'll gradually become more able to receive what your partner tells you with an open mind, without immediately starting to think about how you're going to respond to it. By listening to the other person's painful feelings without feeling attacked, you're also helping the other person to embrace those feelings himself. So this exercise, which at first you should do at least once a day, will eventually influence your communication during the rest of the day. It has such a disarming effect when you never condemn the other person in advance, and take all the responsibility yourself for your feelings. It is so liberating when you stop condemning yourself, and never again have to feel guilty about the other person's feelings. As the autonomy of both partners steadily grows, it forms the basis of an ever-strengthening flow of unconditional love.

Let's now apply this spiritual perspective to a somewhat more serious example, taken from the relationship of Paul and Christine; married for ten years, double income, no kids. Paul notices that one of his female colleagues is showing an interest in him. He doesn't discourage her, as he thinks she's rather attractive. During coffee breaks and work get-togethers they always chat and flirt with each other. At an office party the inevitable moment arrives, and they kiss. She immediately makes it clear that she has no deep intentions with Paul, being married herself, but would very much like to have sex with him. Paul also isn't really in love with her, but finds her very sexy and the idea exceptionally exciting. What's he going to do?

It's obvious that here, in a traditional relationship, a major problem is being generated. After all, the relationship is based on the need for security, and the most insecure situation is when your partner wants to have sex with someone else. This is why many relationships are nailed down with implicit and explicit promises of faithfulness and the absolute ban on extra-relational sex. Even just feeling desire for someone else is taboo, because it's threatening for your own partner. As a result, in the above example Paul will feel guilty about his desire and won't say anything about it to Christine, so that she doesn't get worried and he can avoid her rejecting reaction. But if we're not allowed to feel a feeling, it only gets stronger, so Paul's desire will increase and the ultimate outcome will probably be an affair. All this will have to be kept secret, of course, so dishonesty between Paul and Christine will be added to the mix. It's very noticeable that people who find out that their partner has been having an affair for some time are often more hurt by the sneakiness than by the actual affair itself. They feel 'betrayed' and in fact they have been, although they have contributed to it themselves by consenting to the ban on extra-relational desires.

It's also possible, of course, that Paul could decide to control himself and not have sex with his colleague. To do this, he will have to dissociate from his sexual desires, and if he succeeds, it will seem that the danger has been averted. But those dissociated sexual desires will naturally start to lead a life of their own underground, and will manifest as a loss of self-esteem in Paul, as a buried reproach of Christine, for whose benefit he's suppressed those feelings, and as constantly resurfacing desires for other women, plus the guilt about these. It's possible that this will make the sex with Christine increasingly superficial, or that he'll develop an internet porn addiction. In any event, if Paul stays on the 'straight and narrow' of the traditional relationship in this way, more misery is the inevitable consequence.

This doesn't mean that in a spiritual relationship it's compulsory to have extra-relational sex, or that it always 'must be possible'. It's just that there's no ban on having feelings of any kind whatsoever. And both partners have a strong understanding that they have absolutely no right to the other person, and have no right to forbid each other anything. In a spiritual relationship, then, Paul will tell Christine that he's being seduced by a colleague and finds it exciting. He takes responsibility for the fear that he feels regarding her reaction. She tells him what feelings arise in her: fear of losing Paul, perhaps feelings of inferiority. She takes responsibility for those feelings, starts to work on them herself. Maybe they make a few practical agreements, for example about safe sex, and about what Christine does and doesn't want to know about Paul's adventure. This is all a great relief to Paul, he's been honest about his feelings but wasn't rejected by Christine. He feels tremendous appreciation and admiration for her, because she doesn't burden him with her own fears. It's possible that Paul will now feel so much love for Christine that he shelves the whole plan of having an affair. It isn't actually *so* important, and is it really worth all that agitation?

But maybe Paul does indeed have his adventure, and discovers that there's a big difference between extramarital sex and having sex with your partner. In that case too, his love for Christine will only increase. And yes, of course, there's also a chance that Paul will really fall in love with his adventurous colleague, and end up leaving Christine. But that chance is considerably less than in a traditional relationship, where having sex with someone else is surrounded by all kinds of taboos and prohibitions. You see, marital morality and obligations would be fine if they did actually reduce the chance of misery and increase the chance of happiness. But the opposite is true: they increase the chance that your partner (or you yourself) will run off with someone else, and often that's really the best thing that can happen then, because all that neediness and dependency has already caused the relationship to become suffocating. So wouldn't it be much more valuable if you stayed with your partner of your own free will, simply because that's the nicest thing to do? Which is more important: the secure idea that you'll stay together forever (and a strong chance that in reality this won't happen), or the insecure idea that you can leave each other at any time (and a stronger chance that neither of you will feel any need to do this)? Because as we've seen, the spiritual path is undogmatic and completely free of moral commands and prohibitions. It only looks at the outcome: as much happiness and as little suffering as possible for yourself and others. Monogamy can only contribute to this if it's voluntary and arises out of love and self-esteem, not if it's coerced out of fear and dependency.

The essence of the spiritual path is therefore that you take full responsibility for yourself and for everything that you feel, and don't regard your relationship as a goal in life but as a means to develop that self-responsibility. Your love for each other entails that you can also push each other's deepest buttons of painful, fearful, and dependent feelings. As soon as you stop blaming your partner for those feelings, and learn to feel and embrace them with non-judgemental awareness, your sense of self-esteem and autonomy gets stronger. This self-esteem doesn't depend on other people's love and approval, it's your natural birthright, your inherent natural state of being. One of its by-products is unconditional love. Because each time your partner confronts you with a painful feeling of fear or dependency, anger or frustration, and you succeed in resolving it yourself, this releases not only that inherent self-esteem but also a deep feeling of love. This is pure love, love *an sich*, love without an object. It is unconditional love, and you feel it for everything that lives and exists, including yourself. And therefore, of course, also for your partner, who after all was your 'button-pusher', your access to this unconditional love, and who thus to some extent actually also serves as your 'spiritual teacher'*. This is why you can feel such incredible love and gratitude for your partner in a spiritual relationship. And from this there then flows an effortless considerateness, helpfulness, kindness, and

---

* There is more about the role of the spiritual teacher in Appendix 2.

appreciation. You'll start to indulge each other purely for your own pleasure, without expecting anything in return. This creates a deep connectedness, much stronger than the ties of the traditional relationship, which after all can at most create a semblance of security. A partner like this will never abandon you, because there's simply never any reason to abandon each other. Even if you were to go your separate ways in the future, this would happen lovingly.

If you're in the middle of a relationship crisis at the moment, you have both an advantage and a disadvantage. The advantage is that all kinds of old deep fears and distresses are currently rising to the surface, making it clear that the traditional relationship pattern doesn't work. The disadvantage is that those negative feelings are sometimes so fierce that it isn't possible for a beginner to transform them. What can be done?

It's best to start by releasing each other from all the obligations that ensue from traditional relationship thinking. Stop trying to save your relationship and start trying to save yourself. If your partner shares this way of looking at things, something beautiful can arise from these ruins. But then you must start by giving each other a lot of space. Usually it's best to live apart for a while or, if practical considerations – such as children – make this too difficult, to work in 'shifts': take turns to be away, and spend as much time as possible alone. When fear of losing your partner is no longer your main motivation, greater clarity arises naturally about whether you want to stay together or not. So there's also a strong chance that the relationship will break up. However, perhaps you'll be able to see this not as a failure, but as an opening to give each other and yourself the space for what is really important in your life: the discovery of your natural state. Once the intensity of the painful feelings caused by the separation has subsided, there may even be enough space to develop a new and spiritual friendship or relationship with each other.

If you want to use your relationship crisis as a means to help you on the spiritual path, then the best way to start is with the 'turn-taking talk' described above. In a disturbed relationship, the communication is nearly always disturbed as well, and a highly structured form of communication about your feelings and experiences can offer a way to improve it.

Another aspect that's nearly always disturbed in a relationship crisis is the intimacy. The following exercise can be seen as a kill-or-cure remedy: the intimacy between you will either revive or be completely lost. The first condition for this exercise is that you do it whether you want to or not! It's best to agree a time, put it in your diary, and when the time comes just get started.

Then – without any preamble or 'getting in the mood' – simply take all your clothes off and lie in bed together. You must lie close together, but mustn't do anything else. You've set a kitchen timer for a fixed length of time, such as half an hour, and during that time you must not engage in any form of sex whatsoever: whether coital, oral, manual or any other kind. You're only permitted to feel what's going on inside you, and to occasionally tell each other about this. Cuddling is allowed, but not compulsory. The 'synchronised breathing' technique that will be explained in the next chapter can also be used, if you like. After half an hour the exercise ends. If at that point you both feel like having sex, then you can, but before starting the exercise you must have given each other permission to simply stop at the end of the exercise, regardless of how much the other person might want to have sex.

This exercise helps you to let go of two things: on the one hand, the need to 'be in the mood' before you can experience intimacy, and on the other hand, the idea that if you are 'in the mood' then by definition you must have sex. Strong feelings can arise during this exercise, for example because you're absolutely not in the mood when the exercise starts, or conversely because you desperately want to have sex but it's not permitted (or not possible because your partner wants to stop when the half-hour is up). You can tell each other about all those feelings during the exercise, but must nevertheless resolve them yourself. If you do this exercise a couple of times a week, in combination with the 'turn-taking talk', and you or your partner still hasn't run away screaming, then perhaps you'll be able to transform the relationship crisis into spiritual development. And otherwise, it will at least have become evident more quickly that maybe it's better for you to split up.

By nature, relationships – like everything that exists – are changeable. Everything that exists always changes into something else. There's never something that changes into nothing. Something always disappears by changing into something else. Children become adults. Parents disappear from your life or become good friends. Loved ones die and change into a memory. Strangers change into friends or lovers. What you regard as your 'self' changes constantly, after every experience. In short, everything changes all the time, so relationships do too. Suffering arises when you resist this. It's therefore much better to stop clinging to your partner like your mother's bosom or your father's hand. Let go and change along with the eternal flow of change. Discover that you can feel safe in that constant stream of changes, safe in your perpetually changing self-image, as soon as you stop clinging to it, as soon as you stop identifying with it, as soon as you can observe with non-judgemental awareness and unconditional love. Whether you stay together or not, your relationship crisis is like the cracking of the shell that's always restricted and impeded your freedom and your love. So stop trying to glue it back together, stop amputating yourself and manipulating your partner in the attempt to repair that 'secure' shell. Start living, start loving, discover the inner security that you already had within you, and from which you've always run away in fear, until now. Embrace that fear, because it's the door to your natural state of being.

And what do you do if you're in a relationship with someone who's absolutely not interested in the spiritual path? The funny thing is that it makes almost no difference from the spiritual point of view. When you choose in favour of the spiritual path instead of the relationship as your goal in life, then your attitude towards your partner will change. You'll no longer hold him or her responsible for your own painful feelings, but will resolve them yourself in your non-judgemental awareness. This will make you much kinder and more loving towards your partner. Giving love will become your happiness, regardless of whether your partner returns your love. It's very likely that this will help your partner to become more relaxed. My first teacher on the spiritual path always said, 'No one can resist love, kindness and tenderness for very long.'

It's also possible, of course, that as you become less worried about your own security, your partner will conversely start to feel more insecure, and show increasing opposition to your spiritual approach. In that case, perhaps you can give your partner more confirmation and reassurance. If that doesn't help, the problem will eventually resolve itself, because your partner is unable to function in so much openness, and will look for someone else who *is* willing to participate in a symbiotic security relationship.

Although from a spiritual perspective you're therefore not aiming to save your relationship, you're usually not aiming to end it either, as the solution to your problems. If you end a problematic relationship too quickly, you mostly just take your problems with you into a subsequent relationship, and moreover miss an opportunity to use your problems for spiritual growth. So don't run away from each other too hastily, but rather solve your problems yourself without holding your partner responsible for them, and allow the relationship to simply run its natural course: to flourish or to break up. Both possibilities will then contribute to growth and greater happiness. Only if you have a partner who's entangled in destructiveness will it sometimes be necessary to actively end your relationship. There's more about this in Chapter 21.

So you can see that a choice in favour of spirituality as the most important project in your life immediately solves all kinds of other problems or makes them disappear. If you're not in a relationship, you no longer need to chase after one, which only improves the chance of having fulfilling relationships of all kinds in your life. If you *are* in a relationship, you no longer need to worry about how long it will last: you find security in your own deepest nature, and your relationship flourishes or breaks up, and both are expressions of love. You no longer need to make your partner change to match up to your ideal image ('she doesn't love me as I am') or powerlessly put up with his obstinate flaws ('he's just too easy-going, he's got no drive'). Everything that you experience in your relationship becomes fuel for spiritual practise, allowing your inner self-esteem to burn brightly, and your unconditional love to shine forth. Even breaking off an addictive and destructive relationship then becomes the start of a new life, in which you can only flourish and increasingly express what in reality you are, and always have been: a mind that is perfectly clear and open, radiant with unconditional love.

20

Spiritual sex

Nothing whatsoever is to be removed.
Not the slightest thing is to be added.
Truly looking at truth, truth is seen.
When seen, this is complete liberation.

Asanga, Buddhist teacher in India
(300-370) from: Uttara Tantra

One of the most important aspects in nearly all love relationships is sex. So important, in fact, that the last sentence might be described as 'stating the obvious'. But nevertheless, in traditional love relationships the sex isn't always as good as it could be. The longer the partners have been together, the less they have sex, and the sex itself becomes less surprising and exciting. After the initial period of being in love, the partners gradually lapse into a routine of once a week on Sunday morning (when the children are watching television), or once a month on Saturday night (when the children are staying with their grandparents), or once a year when they're on holiday (after the children have left home). And the sex session starts to follow the same familiar scenario: safe, pleasant, and predictable. It's really quite strange that an activity that is so amazingly pleasurable, and that gives you the opportunity to feel so together, becomes so meaningless and increasingly bogged down in a routine, sometimes even an obligation. People often say it's because of the hectic lifestyle of a young family: busy children, high-pressure job, active social life, there are so many other things to do first that sex gradually fades into the background. But of course the real cause of this phenomenon isn't the lifestyle: after all, especially at such a busy time, you could also choose to make at least one hour of quality time for each other every day. The real cause of this phenomenon lies in the nature of the traditional love relationship: the fact that its main aim is to provide security and keep the fear of rejection covered up. As a result, partners increasingly function as each other's father and mother, which doesn't do much for the excitement level. And as an increasingly fixed pattern gradually arises, the sex becomes less a vehicle for expressing deep feelings and more a security ritual. This makes it even more frightening to deviate from the standard pattern of sex. Many people find it threatening to speak openly about desires and fantasies; if the other person doesn't want to engage in your fantasy, you're going to feel terribly rejected. Sexuality is very closely connected with your deepest feelings of vulnerability, fear and dependency, and in a traditional relationship these must be covered. This is why partners themselves sometimes don't realise for a long time that their love life has become devalued, and continue to bask in the security of each other's love and approval. Until the balance is disturbed, for example, one of them has an affair. This nearly always evokes deep feelings of pain and abandonment, however open-minded you might try to be. And moreover in a traditional relationship you hold the other person responsible for these painful feelings, so you're also immediately faced with a serious relationship crisis.

In a spiritual relationship, the sex is less likely to end up in one of these slowly encroaching routines. After all, both partners are fully aware that too much security is an obstruction to love. They try not to lay claim to each other, and take responsibility themselves for any difficult feelings they may experience. If talking about certain feelings or longings evokes fear of rejection, then this gives them all the more reason to talk about them. As their emotional independence increases, they feel more love, and hence the joyful desire to indulge one another. Because the partners are independent people, and are therefore not using each other to fill the gap of their own feeling of incompleteness, the sex stays just as fresh and adventurous as it was when the relationship began. In short, the sex within a spiritual relationship will reflect the nature of that relationship: open, free, independent and loving, and in harmony with the nature of both partners.

As yet, we're not talking about 'spiritual sex' but about the 'ordinary' way of having sex, which is much more open, adventurous and loving in a spiritual relationship than in a traditional relationship. However, spiritual sex is a completely different way of having sex, which certainly *can* take place within a spiritual love relationship, but also outside of one, for example on a basis of friendship or even without a relationship. It's a way of using sex and sexual energy as a means to help you on the spiritual path. So if you have or are aiming for a spiritual love relationship, it's very useful – although not essential – to also learn how to have sex in the spiritual way. And conversely, if you start to have spiritual sex within a traditional relationship, it's inevitable that your relationship will also become progressively spiritual, open, free, and loving.

I personally discovered the spiritual approach to sex after I'd already been on the spiritual path for a number of years, and for me it was really an amazing revelation! You start to look at sex in a totally different perspective. It was like I'd been using a bicycle to rake the garden all my life, and then one day discovered that you can also ride on it! You can see sex on a biological level as the urge to reproduce, on a physical level as a source of drug-like pleasure, on an emotional level as an expression of feelings, and on a psychological level as a way to cover deep feelings of insecurity and incompleteness. But spiritual sex is the most profound way to have sex: it is a method that allows you to discover and express your natural state of being. In Western literature this method is usually referred to as 'tantra'. This term originally has a much broader and deeper meaning, and encompasses an immensely rich spectrum of spiritual insights and methods, of which working with sexual energy is just one.

If you want to start using sex and sexual energy as a means to help you on the spiritual path, you must first let go of the common misconception that tantra is an Eastern way to 'spice up' your sex life. It's perfectly possible and permissible to use it for that, just like everyone's free to rake their garden with a bike, but it won't do you any good from the spiritual point of view. Only if tantra is part of a training that's aimed at realising the nature of your mind, can the full potential of the techniques be achieved.

Before you can use sex and sexual energy as spiritual training, you first have to understand what's actually going on in the usual method of having sex. Some people will perhaps identify less with the following explanation, because for them sex and emotions are much more intermingled. If this applies to you, then please don't worry that you're not 'doing it right', and you can use the explanation to develop more understanding for people who do actually experience sex and emotions as separate. But anyway, the basic principle of having sex seems simple: first there's arousal, sexual desire, and then there's the satisfaction of that desire via the orgasm. An average sex session starts with spontaneous or artificially generated desire, which is then sustained or increased for a shorter or longer period of time, until an orgasm is the climax and also the end of the session.

Let's now look more closely at the phenomenon of sexual desire. A striking feature is that sexual arousal is experienced very differently within a sex session than outside of one. If you feel strong sexual desire when there's no partner to satisfy you, and it's also not convenient for you to satisfy it yourself, the same desire that's so pleasurable within the sex session is suddenly experienced as something quite oppressive and frustrating. Most men, for example, then do their utmost to obtain the desired partner, or to damned well get rid of that oppressive desire in some other way.

The fact that desire is experienced as something pleasurable during a sex session is therefore, on closer inspection, mainly due to the additional prospect of an orgasm, which is therefore often experienced as a 'release', namely from that desire. For most people, especially for men, a sex session isn't finished if they haven't 'come'. Or even more, without orgasmic release, a sex session has simply been a failure, and also frequently the cause of strong feelings of rejection. So sexual desire is actually only pleasurable when its satisfaction is within reach, for instance if you're having sex with a partner or engaging in masturbation (or self-pleasuring, the term preferred in tantra). In fact, the very word 'satisfaction' indicates that the desire itself is a form of 'dissatisfaction' that you can only eliminate by satisfying it. The fact that the orgasm not only ends the desire, but is also highly pleasurable in itself, just makes it all the more desirable, and therefore even more essential as the end point of that desire. In short, desire is a feeling that in principle we want to get rid of, and this makes it necessary to acquire the object of desire. Or in other words, desire plus our aversion to it make it necessary to strive for the desired object, and make the capturing of that object so pleasurable, because it gives 'release' and 'satisfaction'.

This obsession with the orgasm is seen more often in men than in women, because men are inclined to dissociate from difficult feelings, in this case from sexual need. Women, being inclined to 'merge', are usually more capable of staying present with uncomfortable feelings. This isn't always a sign of advanced spiritual development. Some women give up on their longing for an orgasm because they never get one anyway (often because their partner is too strongly focused on achieving his own orgasm) and compensate for this lack with their willingness to serve the man's orgasm. 'As long as he's happy' then becomes 'as long as he gets an orgasm'. When a woman settles for such an impoverished form of sexuality, this is actually also a form of self-rejection.

It is therefore the aversion to our sexual desire that forces us to seek satisfaction of that desire in the orgasm. If you now replace the word 'aversion' with 'self-rejection', it suddenly becomes clear what actually happens when we strive for satisfaction of our desires. Desire isn't a feeling that exists by itself; it's mixed with a rejection of that feeling, and of the person who feels it: yourself. This is a prime example of our 'need consciousness' in action: as soon as we feel a need or desire, we instantly also feel self-rejection, and we must satisfy the desire in order to cover up that self-rejection.

That link with self-rejection exists in principle with all desires! Anyone who sometimes over-indulges in food or eating sweets, or has some other addiction, can easily confirm this. As soon as a thought is linked to self-rejection, it becomes a compulsive thought, which can only be stopped by satisfaction of the need. The need that is most deeply interwoven with our 'need consciousness' is sexual desire. Deep down, everyone has a rejecting attitude to their own sexual longings. And don't think this is refuted by the 'anything goes' attitude that prevails today in the area of sex. After all, 'anything goes' doesn't relate to sexual desire itself, but to the means of satisfying and eliminating that desire. A few generations ago, there was only one legitimate way to do this: within marriage for the purpose of reproduction. At that time, all other ways had to be more or less secretive. These days, there are no longer any taboos about the various ways to satisfy your sexual desire, and in itself that's a good development, even though this openness results in new problems, such as the commercialisation of sex, compulsiveness, and addiction. But still, it's only when the way you have sex is no longer burdened by taboos and self-condemnation that you can go to a deeper and spiritual level, and also learn to embrace the more subtle rejection of your desires with non-judgemental awareness. Because as soon as we liberate our sexual desire from self-rejection, it reveals itself as an exceptionally powerful energy, as the purest life force, flowing directly from your natural state of being, as the most physical manifestation of unconditional objectless love, as your perfect 'abundance consciousness'!

How do you develop the capacity to 'liberate' sexual desire from self-rejection and transform it into pure energy? The first stage is simply to look very often at what's happening with your own sexual desire. The purpose of the above description isn't to convince you of anything, but to invite you to research this within yourself. For this, it's very important that you also develop and train the instrument with which you conduct this self-analysis: your own observing mind. In this way, training and research can reinforce each other. For example, if you're meditating and you become distracted by sexual fantasies, this isn't a reason to think you're a bad meditator, but a reason to use your sexual desire as the object of your attentive awareness. Look carefully, time after time, at your desire with non-judgemental awareness, and you'll see with increasing clarity your subtle tensing-up, that aversion to your desire, the link with your 'need consciousness', your negative belief. You'll also notice that attentive awareness of your sexual desire sometimes makes that desire subside. This isn't transformation yet, but simply the consequence of the fact that your mind is turning away from your sexual thoughts and focusing instead on the physical sensation of the desire.

If you don't get spontaneous sexual desires during meditation, of course you can also generate them yourself. Think of your most desirable fantasies for a few minutes, until the desire starts to glow in your abdomen. Then shift your attention to the physical sensation, possibly combined with a little attention to your breathing. At the same time, look carefully for that slight resistance to your desire, that need and your subtle aversion to and rejection of it. And don't forget: just look carefully, don't change anything about it!

Another way to practise is during self-pleasuring; alternate fantasising and stimulating with attentive awareness of the physical feeling of desire. You'll notice that each time you do this, your arousal level diminishes. You then have to again utilise new arousing fantasies for a moment. In this way, you alternate the arousing of desire in your thoughts with attentive awareness of the desire in your body. When you're ready for the orgasm, stimulate yourself until the irrevocable start of the orgasm and then do as little as possible while you very attentively allow your mind to look at itself during the orgasm. It also helps if you try to keep your eyes open during the orgasm. Don't forget to enjoy it! Have fun!

When you've been practising this for a while, and you notice that you can stay present with your sexual desire in an increasingly relaxed manner, and can play with your desire to some extent by arousing it and using attentive awareness to make it subside, then you're ready for the next stage. You also do this stage alone. It's really important that you don't start practising with a partner too soon, because then it isn't the tantra technique that transforms your mind, but your mind that changes the tantra technique into a nice little extra that can be added to sex. Don't forget that the spiritual relationship and the spiritual method of having sex aren't ends in themselves, but are means to help you transform your mind, and only as a result of this also become more pleasurable and loving than having sex in the ordinary way. So practise on yourself first!

In the next stage you can start to train in truly transforming your desire. Again, start during your meditation practice. As soon as you feel – spontaneously or deliberately – a strong sexual desire in your abdomen, try to move it upwards through your body. The way to do this is: visualise an intense source of light directly in front of you. For this, Buddhists use a shining visualisation of a Buddha, but it can also be another image that inspires you, or simply a light source that radiates clear, warm light. After a few moments, visualise that this light source enters your abdomen. The desire glowing in your body is now mixed with the radiance of the light source in your abdomen. Then immediately visualise this light source slowly rising upwards through your body. You can assist this by very gently contracting the muscles in your perineum (between anus and genitals) when you inhale.

After some practise, you'll notice that your desire does indeed move upwards, but also that the feeling of neediness completely disappears from it. What at first appeared to be desire, now turns out to be pure energy. When this cloud of energy reaches your heart area, it manifests as pure, objectless love. If you manage to raise this energy even higher in your body, right up to – and even just above – your head, then it manifests as pure, clear awareness. You really must try this sometime; it sounds much more difficult than it is. If you've already been meditating for some time, you'll be able to do it fairly quickly. And if you haven't started to meditate, you can also do this exercise; it will take a bit longer to achieve results, but meanwhile you're actually also training your mind, and therefore killing two birds with one stone.

If you practise this for a while, you'll become progressively relaxed about your sexual desire: you'll see more clearly that desire isn't a problem at all, so it doesn't need to be satisfied, whatever the cost. Gradually, you'll become less obsessed about having an orgasm. Eventually, you'll be able to generate sexual desire in yourself, transform it, and then refrain from an orgasm, and still sleep just as soundly. Only then will you be ready to practise with a partner.

At first, you do this in the same way as you previously did alone. While you're visualising your desire as the clear radiance of a light source, raising it upwards through your body and transforming it into love and clarity, your partner provides a constant supply of new desire. Don't both do this at the same time, but take turns; agree that one of you will stay completely passive and only focus on their own mind and on the transformation of desire, while the other will actively continue to arouse desire. You're naturally permitted to use all imaginable ways of indulging your partner here. After a while, you can reverse the roles. In this way, you can make your foreplay an important spiritual exercise, and also derive more pleasure from it.

It's possible that you'll experience a wide range of reactions to this method of practising. Perhaps you'll find it very difficult to be passive and to allow yourself to be indulged without immediately indulging your partner in return. Perhaps you'll find it embarrassing if your desire completely subsides from time to time, although your partner is really doing his or her very best. Talk about everything that you're feeling, without any judgement whatsoever. You've embarked on a fantastic journey through uncharted territory, and it will only make it more enjoyable if you tell each other about your experiences.

A very special technique that you and your partner can learn together is the wonderful synchronised breathing technique. This can be practised quite separately from sex, with your clothes on. You can use this method any time of day, whenever it's convenient for you both. Start by embracing each other: lying down, sitting, or standing (practise in all three positions). As you embrace, feel each other's breathing. Now try to synchronise your breathing in such a way that when one of you inhales, the other exhales, and vice versa. Breathe through your mouth. When your breathing is more or less synchronised, place your open mouth over your partner's open mouth. Your exhalation flows into your partner as inhalation, your inhalation is your partner's exhalation. At first this sometimes goes wrong, which can result in amusing mishaps where the breathing clashes or you get short of breath. But after practising for some time, you'll increasingly be able to relax into this synchronised breathing. Also try to sometimes keep your eyes open and allow your mind to be conscious of itself. You'll gradually be able to do this relaxed breathing into each other for longer, not too deep and not too shallow, smooth, effortless, no shortness of breath, clear and present in the here and now. Sometimes you'll spontaneously experience a very light and open feeling of love, not so much a love of an 'I' for another, but more a kind of being together in a space that's open and full of love. But don't strive for this, just surrender to the togetherness and enjoy your surrender, your togetherness, and be amazed at how beautiful this exercise is.

I'll explain later how you can combine this method with having sex. But also quite apart from that, and without any sexual desire, you can practise this technique together. When you simply feel love for each other and want to express this, you can breathe together. When one of you feels sadness and the other feels compassion, you can breathe together. When you're both tired and your minds are racing, you can breathe together. When you're walking in the woods and are moved by the beauty of nature, you can breathe together. For one minute, five minutes, ten minutes, as short or as long as you like, you can breathe together. And indeed: you can also breathe together when you're having sex.

When you've practised all these techniques and can do them without needing to think about them too much, you can start to have spiritual sex together. This entails that together you do everything possible to arouse each other (in some spiritual traditions these techniques are described in detail), and whenever you nearly lose yourself in passion and arousal, simply stop and do nothing more.

Relax in that arousal, with your bodies still fully connected. You can alternate a spell of synchronised breathing with a spell of only having eye contact. This will often cause the sexual arousal to diminish, but don't worry about it. Just relax in that total merging. If you like, after a while you can start to move again and together create new arousal, until the desire again flows like fire through your body. And then stop again, relax in that desire, in the togetherness, in completely letting go of any result.

You can also let go of any striving for arousal, and simply stay lying together. The body then sometimes spontaneously takes over from you, and goes into an ecstatic state for which nothing needs to be done; anything that you do obstructs this state.

There's a variant where you visualise the desire as liquid light, and allow it to flow through both your bodies to the rhythm of your breathing. If you're familiar with mantras, you can also use a mantra during this exercise. These are all means to help you lose your old aversion to desire and obsession with orgasm, and transform them into pure, clear, loving energy. But ultimately, when you've practised enough with these methods, you can also throw them out and simply relax in the clear awareness of your desire, and let it spontaneously dissolve into love and clarity.

There's nothing against alternating between spiritual sex and 'ordinary sex'. It's very important that you don't create a kind of ban on having nice 'old-fashioned' sex and an orgasm, because then you're introducing a new form of self-rejection. You can, for example, have ordinary sex one time and the next time have spiritual sex. Or first have spiritual sex and then, after a while, round off the session with a straightforward orgasm. But also allow yourself the fantastic discovery of how wonderful it is to end a sex session without an orgasm: you'll find that you can experience exactly the same fulfilment as after an orgasm, but without the rather exhausted stupor. Instead, you feel a tingling, clear, and loving energy through your body. And this liberation from your orgasm obsession also creates just *so* much freedom and autonomy: the needy orgasm addict becomes the independent bestower of happiness and love. This has a ripple effect on your entire relationship: also outside of sex, you'll be much less needy towards your partner. As a result, you'll also have the courage to be much more open, much more flexible, much more loving. Your 'need consciousness' will ultimately change, once and for all, into 'abundance consciousness', your samsaric relationship will change into a spiritual relationship, and your restrictive identity into an open and generously loving consciousness of your natural state of being. Anyone who thinks that the spiritual path should be nothing but severe discipline and ascetic abstinence must definitely try this method. Discipline then soon changes into joyful regularity, asceticism into being free from neediness. Enjoying yourself in freedom and in complete awareness of your mind is the glorious gateway to your perfect natural state of being.

21

Love derailments

*It is not the appearances that bind you,
it is your attachment to them.*

Tilopa, Buddhist teacher in India
(988-1069)

I explained earlier in this book how the growth of our consciousness stagnates because of identification with our self-image. We saw that identification can take place in two ways: through unconscious merging with a safe pattern, or through more or less conscious dissociation from an unsafe pattern (see Chapter 7). In the area of sexuality and relationships, this results in three different forms of stagnation. Or in other words, there are three ways in which the loving energy from our natural state is derailed by self-rejection and gets stuck in a restrictive pattern of addiction: dissociation leads to sex addiction, merging leads to love addiction, and the interaction between the two leads to relationship addiction.

In fact, of course, everyone who isn't spiritually developed has an addiction to love and approval, which expresses itself as a need for sex, love, and relationships. But within this, it is possible to identify differences of degree. In some cases, the need is so extreme that we can also speak of addiction in the traditional sense of the word. This is characterised by a downward spiral of compulsive and self-destructive behaviour. These three ways in which love becomes derailed are the focus of this chapter.

Sex addiction is rooted in dissociation, and is therefore more common in men than women. The 'dissociator' has developed a mechanism that reacts with lightning speed to (the threat of) painful emotions, namely by pushing them away and focusing attention on pleasant thoughts or activities. However, this also insulates the emotional area, a chronic lack of emotional impulses. This in turn results in a lifestyle aimed at compensating for that lack. In mild form, the 'dissociator' is a restless soul: always busy with new projects, always running away from himself, always searching for enjoyable distraction. In more serious cases, this distraction takes the form of an addiction to one or more elements in the series 'sex, drugs and rock & roll'.

The emotional shielding of the dissociator can be compared to a kind of emotional suit of armour. Pushing away painful emotions means that all emotions are levelled out, and it causes an ever-increasing deprivation of emotional stimuli. That deprivation is compensated with artificial strong emotions, evoked by chemical means or exciting situations, also known as 'kicks'. These have the advantage that they entail only a small chance of rejection. Although sex is very deeply connected with the fear of rejection and self-rejection, the only forms that are addictive are the ones with a minimal chance of rejection, such as using sex workers, anonymous internet sex and pornography. Sex then becomes a 'kick', a strong emotion that can be safely evoked; artificial, it's true, but temporarily very effective as compensation for emotional poverty. It's like driving a car very fast: you don't *really* want to smash yourself up, but the minor chance of this makes the high-speed driving an exciting sensation that gives a brief feeling of emotional satisfaction, a feeling that you're truly alive! That's precisely what the sex addict misses and what he's chasing with his addiction: the feeling of realness, of profound joie de vivre, of vulnerability. And that's precisely what his addiction increasingly takes out of reach.

As a result of these artificially evoked emotions, the 'emotional armour' becomes progressively more impenetrable, the need for kicks more inescapable. Until finally, every day is controlled by this vicious circle. The internet addict must spend hours at his computer every day, chatting or viewing porn, and then each time must release the self-evoked sexual urge by masturbating. And the sex worker addict needs his regular fix of paid sex.

In all these cases, there's an addiction to the excitement, the desire and its release through the orgasm. Without that sexual urge, the sex addict feels empty, emotionless, and lonely. This generates thoughts of sex, which are naturally condemned as weak or bad, depraved or sinful, depending on the belief system in which you were raised. But this only makes them more compulsive: you have to give in to them in order to get rid of the distress. Then the actual sexual urge is evoked: there's excitement, desire, hope and fear, and the prospect of the releasing orgasm. Immediately after the orgasm, there's the stupor of exhaustion. For a moment, your mind is calm, yet there's also a vague feeling of disappointment and self-rejection. Then, after a while, the whole cycle repeats itself. There's a gradual, inexorable increase in emotional poverty and lack of self-esteem, and also in the compulsiveness of the need to repeatedly escape them for a short while.

Can you see how all misery starts with self-rejection? How it's self-rejection that makes our natural life force turn against us and change into oppression and compulsiveness? It's a very understandable mistake that you try to eliminate painful emotions. It's just that the effect is disastrously counterproductive. It's unbelievable how much misery people perpetually cause for themselves and others as a consequence of their attempt to avoid misery.

So if you want to stop a sex addiction, you'll first have to work on the non-judgemental embracing of your sexual desires. Development of your non-judgemental awareness by means of meditation is the best 'cure' in the longer term. In the short term, you can start by trying to no longer reject yourself about the fact that you're addicted. Really, it can happen to anyone, and at a deeper level everyone *is* actually addicted. Addiction creates the most productive misery you could ever wish for: it's a gateway to your spiritual development and to the realisation of your perfect nature. So stop putting yourself down, and instead regard your addiction as an exceptionally instructive mistake. Start by enjoying – without judgement – those sexual activities that you just can't give up. Don't impose a ban on any kind of sexual experience whatsoever. Instead, every time you feel an urge for sexual kicks, look with kindness at the self-rejection that's hidden behind it. Embrace that feeling of discomfort, insecurity, loneliness, disquiet, urgency and desire with your non-judgemental awareness. Very often the urge will then disappear after a few minutes. Develop non-destructive ways to indulge and distract yourself, as an alternative to the compulsive and destructive methods. Take a decision about using the internet or visiting sex workers, or about other situations that evoke a strong destructive desire in you. There's nothing wrong with avoiding those situations, as long as you replace them with different, positive ones. Finally, allow yourself the joy of an open, kind relationship with yourself and with *all* your feelings, whether painful or joyful. In such an open, kind and self-embracing mind, addiction is simply no longer possible.

If sex addiction is thus a symptom of dissociation, a love addiction has its origins in merging with emotional patterns, and is therefore most common in women. It expresses itself as a compulsive attachment to an unrequited or unhappy love. It doesn't matter how hopeless the love might be, and how unattainable the object of the love, the love addict can only keep on loving and hoping for the unattainable loved one. Simply the idea of letting go of the loved one, and abandoning the hope, can evoke strong fear reactions: feelings of overwhelming insecurity and having nothing to hold on to, as if you're in danger of losing every reason for existence. In fact, the unattainable nature of the loved one is an important part of the addiction. The love addict is actually addicted to being rejected. This creates a situation of apparent security, an external 'reason to exist', as a way to fill the absence of an internal reason, a sense of self-esteem. The addiction to being rejected is therefore a very painful form of self-rejection.

In the love addiction, the obsessive feelings of love for the rejecting loved one are the final layers covering a deep sense of existential insecurity. The cause of that basic sense of insecurity usually lies in early childhood, and results from the combination of insecure circumstances and a very dominant and rejecting parent of the opposite sex. If a child feels insecure, and is both protected and rejected by one or both parents, this creates the rather curious link between rejection and security. As long as you're being rejected, at least you're not nobody, not nothing, at least you still have a reason to exist. The unattainable loved one has the same rejecting characteristics as the rejecting parent, and clinging to this loved one is a way to cover the existential fear and insecurity that you learned as a child.

So don't think that love addiction is a symptom of a weak or dependent character. On the contrary, love addicts can also be found among very strong, liberated women, who have worked hard all their lives to keep their fears under control, and as a by-product of that battle have sometimes actually become very successful from the social and professional perspective. They can be very warm and kind to others, but they've just never learned to develop kindness towards themselves, and constantly fall for the 'wrong men': men who are rejecting and have dissociated from their warm feelings.

Here too you can clearly see that it's a powerful quality arising from our perfect nature that's perverted by self-rejection into an oppressive variant. It is unconditional love that appears here in a self-rejecting form: however hurtful and rejecting the loved one might be, this is never a reason to stop loving. The only difference is that in the case of love addiction, the unconditional nature of the love does not arise from the strength and abundance of the natural state, but from the fear and deprivation that are the consequence of merging with a restrictive and insecure self-image. In this way, self-rejection sometimes actually takes on the appearance of its opposite: unconditional love.

A love addiction is difficult to stop. This can usually only be done if the misery that it causes is greater than the existential fear that it has to cover. The danger then remains that after a while you'll again fall in love with another rejecting and unattainable partner. It's therefore better to immediately tackle the deepest cause of your addiction, and develop your inner security, your perfect natural state. Start with the right form of meditation, and choose a therapy or training that helps you to develop a more autonomous sense of self-esteem. When your 'need consciousness' becomes weaker, and you start to catch glimpses of your 'abundance consciousness', then the time is fast-approaching when you'll feel simply too worthwhile in yourself to wait and hope for that other person's love. A mind that knows its own perfect nature can never get addicted again!

If love addiction and sex addiction become entangled – or more precisely: if someone who is strongly 'merged' and someone who is strongly 'dissociated' fall in love with each other – then you get a relationship addiction. As I said, all love relationships are actually a form of addiction to the way your negative belief is covered by your partner's love and approval. But sometimes that mutual dependence is so extreme that one can speak of a relationship addiction not only from a spiritual perspective but also in the traditional sense. Both partners seek in each other a way to cover their own deep fear of abandonment and rejection. The relationship, and especially its reciprocally reassuring effect, is the most important goal in life. The more fearful your partner is, the more you need to inhibit your natural expression in order to reassure him. The more fearful you are yourself, the more you're actually prepared to do that. Also in the sexual area, a relationship of this kind becomes increasingly restrictive. Someone who is really dissociated can only express his feelings through having sex, and in this he has a strong 'orgasm orientation'. Someone who is really merged can only have sex if she feels surrounded by safe emotional warmth.

This antithesis is extremely common – in varying degrees – in traditional love relationships: the dissociated partner needs sex in order to have deeper feelings, the merged partner needs deep feelings in order to have sex. This is why, in such relationships, the man often feels short-changed in terms of sex, and the woman in terms of emotionality, and why the sex becomes a more or less tolerable compromise, in terms of frequency (for the man) and/or intensity (for the woman).

And it's not only in the area of sex that these relationships become a restrictive compromise; an addictive relationship actually gives you very little space to be 'yourself' in any way at all. Or in other words: 'yourself' is just a meagre compromise, a pale reflection of what you'd really like to do and be, a mutilated caricature, made to fit within the narrow limits of the relationship's security.

It's not possible to indicate a clear boundary where the mutual restriction of individuality in the traditional relationship takes the form of a real addiction. In extreme cases, however, it is clearly evident (to outsiders, not usually to the partners themselves!) that fear, compulsiveness and self-destruction play an important part in maintaining the addictive relationship. If one of the partners is addicted to alcohol or drugs, for example, and the other partner clings to the role of rescuer, then this is indisputably a relationship addiction; and also if one of the partners is violent and the other is thus a victim of violence. In general, you can speak of a relationship addiction if the misery within the relationship is much greater than the misery that both partners (and children, if applicable) would have to endure if the relationship broke up. It's astonishing to see the extent to which partners are prepared to put up with misery from each other, simply because they're afraid to lose the seeming security of the relationship.

If you think that you are stuck in a relationship addiction, there is actually only one thing to do: give it up. Earlier in this book I wrote that ending a relationship isn't necessarily the best method for achieving spiritual development. In the case of a truly addicted relationship, however, it is indeed the best method. As soon as a relationship has deteriorated into a form of self-rejection and self-destruction, and therefore into an actual addiction in the narrower sense, it's only by stopping it that you can find yourself again. And also for your addicted partner, your decision to end it is the only – and perhaps indeed the last – thing you can do to help him or her, regardless of how much resistance that decision provokes. All attempts to save the relationship take place within that suffocating context of keeping each other's fear of abandonment and rejection covered up, and are therefore as useful as banging your head on a brick wall. In order to achieve any form of spiritual development, you have to stop that self-destructive head-banging as soon as possible, and end the symbiosis of those two half and fearful egos. It's understandable and completely normal that the very thought of it evokes tremendous fears in you. Try to embrace those fears with non-judgemental awareness, even if it's just a little. The thought of breaking up is actually much more threatening than the break-up itself. So *take* that step, even if it seems to be a step in the dark. Very soon after you've taken that step, it will be as if you're awakening from a nightmare. You'll gradually find yourself again, and you'll be able to start working on your deep fears in a constructive way, so that you won't end up in yet *another* addictive relationship. Only then will you have a clear road towards a happy life, with or without a relationship. But if it's *with* a relationship, then it will be in a loving and fulfilling way, arising out of independence and abundant love, instead of neediness and fear.

This chapter about love derailments could have been much longer, because every addiction – and hence also the sex, love or relationship addiction – consists of highly complex mechanisms that appear at first sight to be very hard to break. The fear of stopping an addiction is one of the most oppressive aspects of the addiction itself. But once you've seen through the addiction, stopping isn't actually difficult at all, but is more a celebration of relief and liberation. My earlier book on addictions (Dutch title *De verslaving voorbij*, not yet published in English; the title translates as *Beyond Addiction*) explains how this can be achieved, and perhaps gives just that extra inspiration to stop the addiction. In the past, I was quite addicted myself (to sex, drugs, relationships and smoking) and can therefore confirm from experience that life beyond all those addictions is really *very* much more pleasant, and that is what I truly wish for you.

22

For the sake of the children

Your children are not your children.
They are the sons and daughters of Life's longing for itself.
They come through you but not from you,
And though they are with you yet they belong not to you.

Khalil Gibran, Lebanese poet
(1883-1931) from: The Prophet

I guess the real reason that my wife and I had children
is the same reason that Napoleon had for invading Russia:
it seemed like a good idea at the time.

Bill Cosby, American comedian/actor

This whole book is about relationships between people in general, and love relationships in particular. Love relationships can be both a major obstacle and a very powerful means to help you on the spiritual path. The same applies for having children. Simply the fact that they take up a tremendous amount of time is in itself a considerable hindrance to spiritual development. And because they're also incredibly sweet and endearing, and at the same time can be exceptionally irritating, self-centred, stupid, tiresome, dependent, and demanding, they're the most effective attention-seekers in the world. But because you love them, they can also help you with learning to embrace your own negative emotions and transform them into spiritual development. In that respect, children are a bit like a spiritual teacher. The function of the teacher is twofold: to inspire and to irritate (more about this in Appendix 2). And your children are especially good at fulfilling that second function, being the most refined button-pushers you'll ever encounter.

So why can both the spiritual teacher and young children push your buttons in such an exceptionally irritating way? It's because they're not attached to their ego: in the case of the teacher, because it has been transcended; and in the case of young children, because their ego hasn't fully developed yet. Consequently, neither the teacher nor young children are particularly impressed by the usual conventions of self-protection. That's why they can sometimes confront you so painfully with your self-protection: your little tricks to guard yourself against rejection and self-rejection. So even if this confrontation comes from your own children, rather than a teacher, it could be very useful as a means to help your spiritual training.

And I emphasise *could*, because parents usually fall into the trap of projection, and hold the child responsible for their own self-rejecting feelings. Parents get a lot of support in this from the prevailing parenting paradigm, which holds them responsible for their children's present and future happiness. This misconception about parenting causes an incredible amount of misery in children's (later) life, and indeed also in the life of the parents themselves. We've already seen that self-rejection is the deepest cause of all our emotional suffering. Well, parenting is the way we pass on our self-rejection to our children. The parenting paradigm makes us believe that children come into the world imperfect and we need to educate them, parent them, so that they become good and happy people.

And as you read that last sentence, you probably feel to some extent, 'That's true though, isn't it? Surely they're not only sweet and cute and lovely, but definitely *also* horribly dependent, irritatingly self-centred, appallingly manipulative and blatantly greedy?!' But no, this feeling is due to those parenting spectacles through which we look at children. Because that is absolutely not what they *are*, they just behave like that from time to time, temporarily, as a way to develop themselves. But because we condemn this dependent, self-centred, and manipulative behaviour in ourselves, and – insofar as we haven't merged with it – have dissociated ourselves from it, we project our self-rejection onto the child who still very openly displays this behaviour. And it's through this rejection that the child develops a belief that she isn't good enough, is weak, dependent, and self-centred, and also learns to cover that belief with socially and morally desirable behaviour.

The idea that we have to teach our children to be happy and civilised is just as deep-rooted as the idea that we have to keep ourselves under control to make sure we don't lapse into bad behaviour. Both ideas spring directly from a negative belief about our nature. The more the parents are stuck in that illusory need for self-control, the more they try to control and manipulate their children towards happy and socially desirable behaviour; which in fact just makes the child believe that he's obviously by nature not good enough, and must first learn to fulfil certain conditions in order to feel worthwhile.

'Yes, but,' you might be thinking, 'surely you can't just leave the little darlings to their own devices?' And indeed, that's not the intention. There is, however, a middle way between manipulation and neglect, between imposing your will on them and abandoning them to their fate, and that way is unconditional love arising from your natural state of being. Just like the sun gives light and heat, unconditional love consists of clarity and warmth. The clarity manifests itself as a clear approach to setting boundaries and providing regularity. The warmth is actually loving embracing, non-judgemental, and unconditional. The wonderful thing is you can only give your children this clarity and warmth to the extent that you also give them to yourself. Or in other words if you're constantly swinging back and forth between self-control and self-neglect in relation to yourself, then you've nothing better to offer your children. But if you have already started to practise letting go of self-rejection, and your mind is already somewhat acquainted with its own perfect natural state, *then* having children suddenly stops being a spiritual obstacle, a sacred duty, a lifelong worry, and a complete loss of your freedom, and becomes something totally different. The relationship with your children then becomes a spiritual relationship, a relationship in which you have as much respect for the autonomy and inherent worth of the other as you have for your own, a relationship in which you make no claim whatsoever to the other, and don't allow yourself to be claimed out of fear of rejection. All the fears and anxieties that are usually such a burden on parenthood then change into joy and inspiration for further spiritual development.

Let's now look at a very specific example from the daily practise of parenting. You're in the supermarket with your child and she's whinging that she wants ice cream. Notice that as a parent you already feel on slightly precarious ground because of all the other people around you: you don't want to look powerless as a parent, although that's sometimes how you feel. Let's say you don't want to give your child ice cream at the moment. This lands you in the standard choice between manipulating or ignoring. You can try to pacify your child with vague promises ('when it's nice weather...'), distract her with difficult tasks ('first find the tin of peas and peanut butter') or threaten her with dire consequences ('if you don't stop whinging right now, you'll *never* get another ice cream *ever* again...'). And when all those tactics have failed, you can switch to ignoring her, marching along the shelves with a grim expression on your face, feeling embarrassed about that awful child whinging and yelling behind you. Notice that in this process you're constantly rejecting both yourself and your child: you feel powerless and a failure as a parent, and you hold your child responsible for this. As a result, of course, the child also feels rejected, which only increases the tendency to whinge. So in both cases, whether you manipulate or ignore, the child is rejected. Yet it's all completely unnecessary: the middle way is so simple, almost too simple to believe.

It naturally begins with the relationship with yourself: you no longer need to be a 'good' parent, so you don't reject yourself and your feelings of uncertainty. If your child then asks for ice cream, you don't automatically have to say no to stop her hassling. Instead, you start by acknowledging her feelings: 'Oh, you'd like ice cream, would you? Ice creams are nice, aren't they? Well, I'm not going to get you one just now, because we're having dinner in about an hour.' Notice that in this way you don't reject either your child or her wish for ice cream, but rather acknowledge both of them with kindness, and still clearly set your boundary. This is an example of that cast-iron combination of unconditional love and crystal-clear boundaries. This is the essence of all effective methods for relating to children. And it actually isn't even a 'method', it's an attitude that arises when rejection and self-rejection have disappeared from your relationship with the child. When you've stopped parenting and have started to look at the here and now, to acknowledge your child in everything she feels and to trust the clarity of your boundaries, then you'll see that the child will also start to behave differently, will reject herself less and will develop more natural (unconditional) self-esteem. It's possible that this won't stop the whinging in all cases, but in fact that's completely unnecessary now. If the child still whinges, it's no longer your problem, because you no longer feel threatened in your position of power as a parent. So you actually don't need to do anything about it, or more strongly, you can even feel compassion for the child in her struggle with painful emotions. And because you don't resist her tantrum, she also learns to let go of it a bit better herself. My earlier book on parenting (Dutch title *Het einde van de opvoeding*, not yet published in English; the title translates as *The End of Parenting*) gives a detailed explanation of this spiritual way of relating to your children.

In a spiritual relationship you don't lay any claim whatsoever to the other person, you have no right to the other person, and you alone are responsible for your painful feelings. Having children seems to conflict with this. After all, the general opinion is that if you have children, you – as parents – should never split up, because that is very harmful for the children. It is indeed true that children with divorced or separated parents are on average more likely to have emotional problems than children who haven't been through a separation. But it's difficult to determine whether this is due to the separation itself, or to the distressing period of parental conflict that precedes and also often follows it. Trying to protect your child from difficult situations, whatever the cost, creates fear and lack of self-confidence in the child. Instead of this, it's better if you learn how to handle difficult situations and emotions. You will then automatically pass *that* on to your children.

If you have children, then you have an exceptional opportunity to stop passing on your self-rejection to the next generation. It's fantastic, of course, if you can do this together with your partner in a relationship that's aimed at autonomy and ending self-rejection. But if that isn't possible, and the relationship has become a source of additional misery, a mutually oppressive trap of rejection and self-rejection, then it's fairly pointless to stay together 'for the sake of the children'. It's naturally important that you first try everything to together transform your relationship misery into an aid to your development. But if it's no longer possible to engage in kind or loving communication, if there's no longer any mutual respect, no prospect of love and openness, then give your children the best you can still give them, and split up. Give them two co-parents who live apart and are happy, instead of a pair of angry, miserable people who resentfully stay together. Don't use your children as an excuse not to choose in favour of yourself, or as a cover for your fear of being alone, because then you only give them dependence and fear as a self-image. Let them share in your spiritual adventure, the quest for your perfect nature, the dissolving of your self-rejection, preferably together with your partner, and – if that isn't possible – then each separately, but let them share in the most wonderful thing you can ever give yourself: yourself.

23

The perfect illusion

Form is Emptiness,
Emptiness also is Form.
Form is no other than Emptiness,
Emptiness is no other than Form.

> Heart Sutra, Buddhist scripture

From what is not manifest
All manifestations arise.

> Dynamic Energy of the Lion Tantra

Without something, what fun is it to be nothing?

> Byron Katie

Reflecting on the long and complex series of mistakes that form our identity and almost determine everything we do, you might be inclined to adopt an aggrieved or resentful attitude, along the lines of 'What a horrible world this is! Why does it all have to be so complicated and painful, why can't we all just be happy'? Completely understandable: you're then looking at the mistakes through the spectacles of those mistakes. Or in other words: you're rejecting the rejection. You're condemning the condemnation. Do you recognise here the subtle trap of dissociation? Rejecting the system of rejection is still a form of rejection, so it doesn't help you at all. And in fact it's completely unnecessary, because in reality all those mistakes are part of a perfect system of mistakes, a perfect illusion. As long as you think that reality isn't good as it is, you've forgotten that it's your way of looking that isn't good. The perfect reality then lets you know about this mistake, in a very insistent manner.

Each time you feel aversion to a situation or a person, or to yourself, it's your non-judgemental awareness that is forgetting itself and allowing itself to be swept along in its own projection. And each time you make that mistake, it's immediately brought to your attention: you feel pain. And if you then make the mistake of running away from that pain, you get another warning: you feel even more pain. It's an infallible system. And each time you cling to a situation or a person that fills you with happiness, and you become attached to the self-esteem that this gives you, it's your perfect abundance consciousness that allows itself to be swept along in the illusion of neediness. Each time you make that mistake, it's immediately brought to your attention: it evokes fear, fear of losing that person or situation, fear of rejection and self-rejection. It's an infallible system.

Have you ever sat outdoors on a warm summer night, gazing at the stars, and felt a sense of amazement and awe at the vast expanse and diversity of the universe? In fact, it's all much more awesome than that! As soon as you stop looking through the spectacles of preference and rejection, and start looking from your non-judgemental, loving, natural state, all of reality shows itself in its true nature: a varied and immeasurable assortment of images, sounds, events, thoughts and feelings, so perfectly complex and infinitely extensive that the ecstasy you feel is literally mind-blowing. You see yourself playing a part in that 3D movie with images and sounds, with smell, taste, and touch, and a succession of subtitles in your head. Fascinated, you watch as a hand that you know to be yours pours hot water into a teapot, while another hand (also yours) holds the string of the teabag. Enthralled, you follow your own story: are you going to read a book? Or maybe go for a walk first? And how delightful to have eye contact with another being, and to recognise your own perfect nature again in that being. What a joy to love yourself and the other without distinction, with the love arising from that abundant nature. Compliments and reproaches, approval or rejection, success or failure, even pleasure and pain, they all start to have the same taste of a perfect illusion, and you experience them with the same undertone of exuberant joy. This is the perfect state of being that already was and is and will be. The Tibetan term for this realisation – and the teaching about it – is *Dzogpa Chenpo* ('the great perfection'), or in short: *Dzogchen*. All suffering arises from ignorance and the denial of this perfect state. As long as you're unable to see the perfection of reality, you will be alerted to this in a perfect way, time after time, by means of fear and pain. Only when you finally see the perfection of fear and pain will suffering change into realisation, into profound joy about that perfection, into love and gratitude for the teachers and the timeless knowledge that brought you to this point, and into warm-hearted compassion for everyone who has not yet recognised this perfect, joyful state.

The perfect reality, the nature of the mind and of all things, is an infinitely extensive openness of awareness. This knowing, aware quality loses itself in its own stream of thoughts and is then experienced as an 'I', a 'self', a subject. At the same time, the substanceless stream of sensory perceptions is experienced in the awareness as a reality that actually exists outside the 'self', as an object. Subject and object are wrongly regarded as real entities that exist independently of each other. This is the mental state in which most of us live.

In reality, however, subject and object are not two separate entities, but rather they together form a constantly changing experience in the open space of the perfect mind. So why can't we see that? Because of thinking! Look at how subtly it works: we believe (think!) that it's reality that causes our problems and misery, and this makes us resist it and engage in even more thinking in order to find a way out of that misery. But in fact it's this thought that causes our suffering! The idea that our thoughts relate to how reality truly is, is itself nothing more than a thought, a projection of the thinking mind! And that this projection is really true, is in turn just another thought. The whole experience of an 'I' that is hurt and a 'reality' that does the hurting takes place solely within the experiencing mind. You see, even the most terrible experience takes place in that open, aware nature of the mind, but we just don't realise it because that aware mind has lost itself in its own stream of thoughts and sensory experiences. So look at your mind and see that what is looking is also that which is being looked at! The great Dzogchen teacher Longchenpa (14th century) wrote, 'Recognise awareness in observing it'. See also that when you look at your mind, you're seeing nothing other than what you already saw before: observations, thoughts, and feelings. Yet there's a world of difference between seeing reality as a real oppression, with yourself as its powerless victim, and seeing reality as a transitory stream of experiences in the perfect mind, and yourself as that perfect mind. It is the difference between suffering and perfection, between samsara and nirvana.

When you learn to look at reality and see that mind and experience are a perfect unity, then you'll increasingly recognise the perfection in every apparent imperfection; for instance, in those two major obstacles on the spiritual path: merging with safe patterns of thinking and dissociation from unsafe patterns. In these, you can now recognise the two most important qualities of the mind's perfect nature: the ability to embrace reality with loving awareness and to transcend it with clear awareness. Without awareness, loving embracing is mutilated into merging, and clear transcendence into dissociation. But when these qualities function within the clarity of the perfect self-knowing awareness, they form the dyad of all spiritual growth: transcending and embracing, wisdom and love.

You can examine in yourself how subtly this mechanism works. It can sometimes be seen when you're alone and have been watching television or reading for a while. You've been distracted from the here and now for quite a long period of time, and have been merged with the events in the movie or book. Then at a certain point the movie ends or you finish the book. The temporary state of merging stops abruptly, and you briefly become conscious of yourself in the here and now. Observe carefully: you might now experience an uncomfortable feeling. This is the most subtle self-rejection, inherent to being distracted from your aware state. And it's accompanied by the urge to immediately start doing something else. If you have little or no meditation experience, you won't recognise this urge and will therefore give in to it immediately: you'll start zapping channels or reading something else, or immediately go to bed or whatever. You dissociate from the uncomfortable feeling. But if you've been meditating for a while, and you recognise the subtle self-rejection and can stay present with it for a few moments, embracing it with non-judgemental awareness, then dissociation changes into transcendence to a clearer and more spacious self-knowing awareness. When self-rejection is lovingly embraced, it is transcended in clear, non-judgemental awareness. Each time awareness finds itself again in this way, it becomes a little clearer and more stable, and thus more able to embrace the next manifestation of self-rejection or despair with even more loving awareness. In the end, this process of embracing and transcending becomes simultaneous and effortless: after all, they are two sides of the same perfect mind. As soon as the negative feeling arises, it is immediately recognised and embraced. It liberates itself in the open and loving state of the mind's nature and is then experienced as love and clarity.

In this way, our perfect nature – the Buddha in each of us – is distracted and swept along by its own projections, and thus becomes alienated from itself. Each time we're confronted with this, we feel uncomfortable and out-of-place in that alienated state of being. And then we quickly run away from that feeling into a new distraction. This is the vicious circle of samsara, the self-sustaining mental suffering. Each time we're trapped in self-rejection, it's the inner Buddha who wants to be freed, and is hammering painfully hard on our door. And time after time we keep the door closed, and run away from ourselves into a new distraction; completely understandable, but not at all practical.

In the end, it gradually dawns on you that this strategy isn't working. You've had enough of going round and round in circles. It's only when we see that we ourselves are responsible for our own suffering that we start to train our mind in looking at itself, searching for our own nature. And it's only then that the miracle is revealed! Only then that the discomfort and self-rejection turn out in reality to be the gateway to our perfect nature. Then our suffering turns out to be the unrequited love of our perfect nature for our straying mind. Then the snake turns out to be only a piece of rope, and we can safely go back into our own house, and start to live in and from our own perfect nature.

That is the essence of meditation: learning to look at your mind, to recognise when you're being distracted, to experience the subtle uncomfortable feeling about that; seeing your tendency to dissociate from that uncomfortable feeling, and then simply not doing it, and instead continuing to look, being distracted time after time and recognising it as merging, the mutilated version of a loving embracing, continuing to look and thus embracing ever subtler layers of self-rejection with loving awareness. As a result, the tendency towards merging and dissociation will dissolve into its own natural state: the all-transcending clarity of the self-recognising awareness, the open, clear and loving natural state. Transcending and embracing. Clear and loving. Light and warmth. So simple. So beautiful.

A fungus that was recently found in the United States has spread over an area of more than 3.5 square miles. The *Armillaria* fungus is an underground system of root-like filaments with many branches up to the surface, where it becomes visible as a kind of mushroom. This fungus and the thousands of little mushrooms that sprout up from it are therefore one single organism. If all those individual mushrooms could think, they would naturally see themselves as separate beings. They would identify with their singular form, not with their collective nature. And they would naturally also see the other mushrooms as separate beings, and fall in love with some of them, be angry with others (or the same ones), and simply be indifferent to most of them.

This is how, in reality, we are connected as human beings. In our deepest essence, we are one single perfect 'mind' that joyfully expresses itself in countless manifestations. And then loses itself in them, by completely identifying with its own manifestation. Look again at the depiction of our identity in Figure 1 on page 7. All the layers of our self-image enclose our natural state of being. That is our 'Buddha nature', and in the figure it's left as white as the paper on which it's printed. But outside those layers it's also white: everything that we perceive as 'outside ourselves' is also a manifestation of that perfect state of being. Other creatures are that too. As soon as the layers of our identity dissolve into non-judgemental awareness, the white space within them is no longer different from the white space outside them. Is the space inside an empty bottle different from the space outside it, when the bottle is broken?

You see: we're searching for our own perfect nature, but when we find it we realise it was always already the nature of everything – the unbounded, self-aware space in which everything is a joyful manifestation of that clear, loving nature. And the wonderful thing is: you are still yourself, you do your things, you love your loved ones, you go to work, you stub your toe in the shower, you enjoy your chocolate dessert. But at the same time, everything is illuminated by the joyful undertone of non-judgemental awareness. You are still yourself, but without that illusion of separateness from everything else. Instead, you are one with everything that you see and hear and think and feel. 'Yourself' is an experience just like all the others, and in everything there's that unshakeable basis of love and clarity, that constant undertone of joy and humour. It's completely understandable that we're accustomed to seeing our 'self' as the centre of a truly existing reality that surrounds us. In the same way, people used to think that the sun and the stars revolved around the earth. But what a liberating realisation that you don't have to keep the universe under control, that you don't need to protect your 'self', that you can just 'be', along with everything else, without needing to fulfil even one single condition.

Our deepest longing for a perfect love relationship, for 'the one' who totally loves us and accepts us as we are and will never leave us, turns out to be a projection of what in reality we already are! No one can ever give you what you are already. That's why relationships based on 'need consciousness' can never bring the happiness that you seek from them. When you realise this, you can live in love without relationships based on neediness, and instead will share your abundance with others, in any form of relationship whatsoever. There is no greater happiness, no warmer love, no clearer insight, no more intimate togetherness, no truer autonomy, no more powerful self-esteem than this. This is what you are and always already were and forever will be: *Dzogchen*, the great perfection.

This was my explanation of the mother of all mistakes: the denial of our perfect, abundant, natural state of being. And of course it's not my own story, but an age-old wisdom that is supplied as a user manual with life, and that underlies many different religions and spiritual traditions. Insofar as I have understood that age-old wisdom, I have tried to present it in my own words, so that I can perhaps be of service to you as a fellow traveller on this spiritual voyage of discovery. If this wisdom has lost any of its authenticity and purity in this attempt, then that is entirely my responsibility. I sincerely hope and wish that this book has inspired you to go further on this spiritual path and seek the advice of an authentic spiritual teacher or tradition, and especially to start training your mind to recognise its own perfect nature. May this book contribute to a reduction in suffering and an increase in happiness and love in the world.

APPENDIX 1

Sources, recommendations and thanks

> *Does the moon*
> *Glide past*
> *Without purpose?*
> *It is a messenger, warning*
> *That your life is passing by.*
>
> Zen poem

This book developed over a period of several years and derives influences, both great and small, from many different sources. The most important of these is undoubtedly Tibetan Buddhism, which I have been studying and practising since 1998. The book that brought me into contact with this ancient wisdom is *The Tibetan Book of Living and Dying* by Sogyal Rinpoche, a Tibetan lama who has lived in the West for over thirty years. He studied comparative religion in England and now teaches all round the world. Quite soon after reading his book, I went to his retreat centre in the south of France to study with him, and since then he has been my main teacher. It is from him and from his teachings on the vision and practice of Buddhism that I constantly draw inspiration, and am learning to see that we are all manifestations of the perfect natural state of being. Rinpoche is for me the conclusive proof that it really is possible to transcend your limiting self-image and live from within the effortlessly flowing love and clarity of the natural state.

If you seriously want to train your mind in the spiritual way, then I recommend that you take a meditation course offered by one of the many Buddhist traditions represented in the UK and other European countries. Each of them has a slightly different approach, its own style and character, and you can take a look around and attend open days to help you choose. The method that I've described in this book comes from the *Dzogchen* approach to Buddhism, which is only taught within Tibetan Buddhism. A related method that is also taught in Tibetan Buddhism is *Mahamudra*. There are various Tibetan Buddhist centres in the UK that give meditation courses, including the Rigpa centres of Sogyal Rinpoche. You can find more information about Rigpa around the world at www.rigpa.org.

In Appendix 2, I write about the effective combination of Eastern spirituality and Western training techniques. I learnt many of those Western techniques at the Essence organisation in Amsterdam, where I followed an intensive training programme between 1995 and 2000. There are also several Western training institutes where you can learn to let go of negative self-rejecting patterns and acquire positive patterns. These are not – in themselves – spiritual training programmes, because they don't teach how the mind can get to know its own perfect nature. But they *can* help you to work very effectively on inhibitions and blocks, and develop a more positive and healthy self-image. I look back on that period of training with great pleasure and gratitude, and especially to Michal Perl from Haifa, who was my main trainer. She was the first teacher who helped me to catch a glimpse of my own perfect nature, and she remains a wonderful example through the complete and loving dedication with which she offers her knowledge and experience in the service of other people's development.

If you'd like to practise with the tantra method, there are many tantra institutes to choose from. Most of them are Western organisations that make the Eastern tantra techniques accessible to Western people. In some cases, part of the original spiritual context is lost, which means that for many people Western tantra is restricted to a training course in loving and ecstatic sexual practices. But if you provide the spiritual context yourself, a Western tantra course can be an excellent way to learn the necessary techniques. I personally did a beginner's course at the Centre for Tantra in Amsterdam, run by Carla Verberk and Remmelt van Kleef, and I have very happy memories of it. They truly create an atmosphere of kindness, safety, and integrity in their training courses.

A good, comprehensive book about tantric love is: *The Art of Sexual Ecstasy: The Path of Sacred Sexuality for Western Lovers* by Margot Anand (ISBN 978-0874775815).

There are currently few Western spiritual teachers who write very inspiring books about their own enlightenment experience, but don't really explain how you can achieve such a splendid state of realisation yourself. An exception to these is the American writer Byron Katie. She has developed a wonderfully simple method, known as *The Work*, which is a great way to learn how to see through your oppressive negative concepts, and stop projecting them onto other people and your circumstances. You can learn how to live in harmony with the way things are. Her standard book (with co-author Stephen Mitchell) is: *Loving What Is: Four Questions That Can Change Your Life* (ISBN 978-0712629300). Another interesting and illuminating book by her (with co-author Michael Katz) is *I Need Your Love – Is That True?* (ISBN 978-1844130269). She also gives workshops, mostly in the U.S. and Europe (including London). See www.thework.com.

In the process of breaking free from self-rejection, I was greatly helped by the book *Soul Without Shame* by the American writer Byron Brown (ISBN 978-1570623837), and a three-day workshop with him. The book gives a clear insight into the functioning of a typical aspect of our self-rejection, namely our inner critic or judge, the internalised voice of our parents that tells us what we can and can't do, and is sometimes a very heavy burden to bear. It contains a wide range of practical exercises. I sometimes give a workshop myself with the title (translated into English) 'Free from the Inner Critic', which covers material of – among others – Byron Brown.

I have also been greatly inspired by the work of the American philosopher and Buddhist Ken Wilber (see also Appendix 2). As a philosopher, he has done excellent work in uniting science and spirituality. His book *A Brief History of Everything* is a good introduction to his philosophical work (ISBN 978-0717132331). As a spiritual practitioner, he has given very clear and inspiring descriptions of his experiences on the spiritual path. This aspect of his writing is clearly expressed in, for instance, his book *The Simple Feeling of Being* (ISBN 978-1590301517). I find his more recent work on 'integral spirituality' rather more difficult to follow, because of its highly detailed nature.

The array of Buddhist books that have inspired me is simply too extensive to mention. Also everyone should find their own way in this area. However, just to give some idea, I will name one or two authentic Buddhist teachers who are also very accessible for Western students. Yongey Mingyur Rinpoche is a young Tibetan monk who has written an exceptional book *The Joy of Living*, an introduction to Buddhism and meditation, with interesting references to relevant scientific research (ISBN 978-0553824438). His brother Tsoknyi Rinpoche has written several very accessible books about Dzogchen. His first book is called *Carefree Dignity* (ISBN 978-9627341321). Another young Tibetan teacher is Dzongsar Jamyang Khyentse, whose book *What Makes You (Not) a Buddhist* gives a refreshingly original introduction to Buddhism (ISBN 978-1590305706). A Tibetan teacher from an older generation is Namkhai Norbu, one of the last lamas to grow up in Tibet. However, he speaks English quite well and often teaches about *Dzogchen: the Self-Perfected State*. This is the title of one of his books, which is a good introduction to this highest form of meditation instruction (ISBN 978-1559390576). Then there is the Vietnamese monk Thich Nhat Hanh, who has written many books about Buddhism, too numerous to list, which are all highly accessible. All these teachers visit Europe from time to time, and it can be wonderfully inspiring to attend their lectures and teaching events.

If, after reading this book, you think that I can personally help you in any way, or if you'd simply like to respond to what I've said, then you're most welcome to contact me via my website www.jangeurtz.nl. Although I am not a therapist or spiritual teacher, as a coach and fellow traveller on the spiritual path I sometimes give workshops or individual consultations. You'll find more information about this on my website.

It only remains for me to thank everyone who helped me in writing this book. Most of it was written during a six-month retreat at Lerab Ling in the south of France, and I am very grateful for the friendship of the other retreatants, and for the many discussions I had with them about spirituality, especially Karel Lefèvre and Eric Soyeux. I am extremely grateful to my test readers: Linde Geurtz (my daughter), Marc Matthijsen and Suzanne Kooij. They all, each from their own angle, gave highly valuable feedback on the manuscript, and thus contributed greatly to this book.

All my love and gratitude go to my spiritual life partner, with whom I have learned to love in the spiritual way, and who constantly inspired me with her love and friendship during the writing of this book.

It is perhaps rather unusual, but I would also like to thank myself very much for writing this book, because although it will perhaps be useful to others, I myself have certainly learnt a great deal from it. There is truly nothing in the world more inspiring, enjoyable, and instructive than to receive, and then to pass on spiritual knowledge and experience. My wish is that everyone may have that joy.

Lerab Ling/Amsterdam, 2008

APPENDIX 2

Western resistance to Eastern spirituality

If there is any religion that could cope with modern scientific needs, it would be Buddhism.

Albert Einstein, German-American physicist
(1879-1955)

In my work as a meditation instructor, I've often found that although people feel attracted to spirituality, they also feel quite wary of actually following a spiritual path. This often has something to do with certain aspects of Eastern spirituality that meet resistance in the Western mind. The most serious resistance stems from the notion that spirituality is very airy-fairy, a kind of belief that's based only on wishful thinking, and is therefore actually nothing more than an escape from scientific reality. The main reason for this misunderstanding is what philosophers call the 'pre/trans fallacy'. The way this works is: from early childhood, everyone goes through a development that comprises different phases or stages. The child's consciousness develops from a physical stage, via a magical stage (evil monsters and good fairies), an emotional stage and various rational stages of concrete, formal and abstract thinking, into an adult form of social rationality that is capable of transcending immediate self-interest.

If we look at the historical development of all humankind, we see that the group consciousness or 'level of thinking' of a people or society also develops via such phases or stages. Primitive peoples first had only a physical consciousness, like that of animals. After this, there arose a magical and mythical consciousness: magical power and all kinds of gods and invisible spirits had an influence on daily life. The development proceeded further via emotional stages (family consciousness, tribe consciousness, national consciousness) to the rational stage that is currently under development, in which the dawning of global consciousness is taking place, and a growing realisation of the equality of all beings (as expressed by the United Nations, not so long ago, in the Universal Declaration of Human Rights).

'Spiritual science' proposes – and for some people has proved – that further stages of growth are possible, in both individual consciousness and the consciousness of humanity as a whole. These are the realisation of the 'emptiness' or non-substantial character of all beings and phenomena (*shunyata*), the realisation of the individual perfect nature (the 'nature of the mind') and the realisation of the connectedness of all that exists (non-dualism). These three highest stages thus go beyond the rational stage, and are therefore known as 'transcendent' or 'transrational'. So the entire sequence of developmental stages, of both an individual and a society, can be summarised as pre-rational stages (physical, magical, mythical, emotional), rational stages (concrete, formal, abstract) and transrational stages (shunyata, nature of the mind, non-dualism). This outline of the different stages that I have just given is very concise and inexact; a much better and more detailed description is given by the American philosopher Ken Wilber (see also Appendix 1).

The pre/trans fallacy arises when something that is pre-rational is mistakenly seen as transrational, or conversely something transrational is seen as pre-rational. Many people, and scientists in particular, look at spirituality without having any personal knowledge of those transrational stages, so they mistakenly see all forms of spirituality as pre-rational, hence irrational, hence nonsense and baloney. Their misconception is strongly confirmed by many others who make the opposite mistake, thinking that they are practising transrational spirituality while in reality they are engaging in pre-rational activities. This quasi-spirituality sometimes takes place in the traditional religious field, and very often in a wide variety of contemporary New Age forms, ranging from emotional manipulations that evoke a feeling of connectedness or profundity by means of group sessions in mantra recitation, trance-dance, sweat lodges and fire ceremonies, to ecstatic experiences with sex and drugs. There's nothing wrong with any of these, and sometimes they're actually very pleasant, but as long as these experiences are an end in themselves, and therefore not related to the transrational aspects of consciousness, not aimed at realisation of the perfect state of being, this is not spirituality in the deepest sense of the word.

A very common pre/trans fallacy was mentioned earlier in this book: the misconception that children are in a natural state of being; that as adults we have lost that state, and we must go back to it in order to accomplish our spiritual path. Here, the pre-rational state of the child (in which the ego is still in the process of developing) is confused with the transrational state of egolessness.

Conversely, a pre/trans fallacy occurs if you think that a Buddhist practitioner who has sunk into a conceptless meditation (transrational meditation) is engaged in 'navel-gazing' (pre-rational obsession with one's own emotions).

In a balanced spiritual path, all the stages are integrated. When you're on a balanced spiritual path, you don't try to dissociate from pre-rational aspects of your development, but embrace them in awareness and integrate them in your spiritual practice. A healthy physical condition and balanced emotional life contribute to your spiritual development. Religious aspects such as rituals and prayers can also play a part on the spiritual path, as long as they're integrated with the transrational aspects. If they are separate from these, then all you're doing is participating in religious activities. Again, there's nothing wrong with this; religious practice can, for example, inspire someone to abstain from negative actions and develop positive ones, which contribute to more happiness and less suffering, and as such is not irrational. But without the transrational perspective, it does not lead to realisation of the natural state of being and is therefore essentially not a spiritual path.

In addition to this pre/trans fallacy, there is another reason why, in the Western world, spirituality is often mistaken for airy-fairy nonsense. The tremendously successful scientific developments of the last century, together with the almost total collapse of the Christian religion, have resulted in a new kind of 'rational religion': science. And in precisely the same way as many individuals in their development try to dissociate from a certain stage once they've transcended it, Western society – after almost two thousand years of Christian religion – has switched to dissociating from its religious stage. Many people in the West have thus developed 'religiophobia': as soon as anyone starts singing hymns or mantras, performing rituals, or in some other way striving for 'higher things', the sceptical mind is ready and waiting to cut down this twaddle with sharp arguments. Of course there really are some charlatans, bogus gurus, and fake saints, and it's very good that they're exposed. Unfortunately, the criteria are purely scientific-rational (and sometimes also purely emotional-aversive), so not only pre-rational aberrations but also every authentic pre-rational and transrational form of spirituality is rejected as unscientific. The logical error that's always made here is to take the absence of scientific proof that a phenomenon or viewpoint is true as proof that it is untrue. However, there are some phenomena, such as the transrational stages of our development that *a priori* cannot be scientifically proved, because they fall outside the rational and conceptual realm of science.

Yet it is sometimes possible to rationally prove that these transrational phenomena are not in conflict with reason. Recent scientific research into the effects of long-term meditation on the brain has shown that the parts of the brain where feelings of happiness and security are located become clearly larger under the influence of meditation – and not only during meditation but also afterwards. The change is therefore of a lasting nature. For people who meditate, such research is only an added bonus, because after all they personally experience the positive effect on their health and emotional life.

But scientific publications of this kind can indeed help to diminish the pre/trans fallacy and increase society's interest in an authentic spiritual path.

A great deal of Eastern spiritual knowledge is mixed with pre-rational culture and religion of its country of origin. Tibetan Buddhism is a good example of this: its religious aspects come from pre-rational shamanism (magical stage), a religion that was practised for centuries in Tibet before mixing with the Buddhism that was imported at a later date from India. Individual practitioners in Tibet had no problem integrating those pre-rational aspects, which after all were learnt at their mother's knee, within the rational and transrational practice of Buddhism. The pre-rational religiousness thus served in Tibet as an effective aid in realisation of the higher transrational stages of spirituality.

But if a pre-rational religion is offered to Western adults, who are in a rational stage in terms of both individual and societal development, then the pre/trans fallacy will often come into action in two different ways. A large group of rationally minded Westerners who are dissociated from their magical and religious stage will reject Tibetan Buddhism since they fail to recognise the transrational wisdom because it is mixed with pre-rational religion: 'If it says you have to perform offering rituals, then it can't be true spirituality'. Which is most unfortunate: they throw out the precious gift of spiritual knowledge with the religious packaging that they find unattractive.

A smaller group of Westerners, namely those who are still somewhat merged with their religious stage, make the opposite mistake and regard the pre-rational aspects as transrational, so they are seen as a 'higher' truth than they actually are. Shamanist practice is therefore mistaken for spiritual practice; these people think that the rituals in themselves lead to enlightenment, thus giving priority to the religious form over the spiritual substance. The real transrational knowledge is ignored, or – if it is indeed noticed – still approached in a religious way: a lot of belief but not much personal research into whether it is true.

In both cases, there is a spiritual obstacle. The rational 'religiophobes' can overcome this obstacle by letting go of their dissociation from pre-rational religiousness and investigating which religious aspects they could perhaps use on the spiritual path. For the religious Buddhists, the best way might be to test out their belief by studying and conducting 'spiritual-scientific' research; that is to say, practising meditation alongside or instead of the religious liturgical practice.

There could perhaps be another reason why many Western people hesitate to take a spiritual path. This is because it seems that you must start by renouncing a lot of the nice things in life, and instead must subject yourself to years of strenuous training, meditating for hours on end every day, while moreover the end result – enlightenment – seems quite vague and *very* far away. This is an understandable mistake, and in fact is part of the very problem for which the spiritual path offers a solution. The same distortion of reality is experienced by everyone who thinks about stopping smoking or some other addiction. Although the addiction has actually already caused a vast amount of misery in your life, the idea of stopping immediately evokes the fear that life after the addiction will be much more dull and boring, devoid of any kind of pleasure and enjoyment. This fear and hopelessness are part of the addiction illusion. The reality is the opposite: it is the addiction that causes misery and oppression, and freeing yourself from it gives tremendous joy and actually makes your life much more pleasant.

In the same way, thinking about a more spiritual way of life also evokes fear that life will then become more boring, that you'll never be allowed to go slightly wild ever again, that you'll only be allowed to sit meditating on a cushion, very seriously and with great self-discipline. The reality is the opposite: spirituality is liberating; it frees you from your addiction to other people's love and approval, it frees you from your compulsive tensing-up reaction to reality and your own feelings, and it creates a state of love and happiness which is beyond comparison.

Another aspect of the spiritual path that is often misunderstood by Westerners is the phenomenon of the spiritual teacher. After two thousand years of religious domination by the Roman Catholic church and its countless breakaway Christian denominations, most people have had quite enough of obedience and submissiveness, and it seems that this is precisely what is required again by a spiritual teacher. We all know examples of sects where things have gone very wrong with that obedience, culminating in mass hysteria or group suicide. We are therefore very mistrustful of following a spiritual teacher, and in itself that is completely justified. But there are also significant advantages of having an authentic spiritual teacher. Because although you can still practise spirituality without a teacher, your progress will be much faster if you have one. There are two reasons for this.

First, it is wonderfully inspiring to become acquainted with someone who is much further along the spiritual path than yourself. The teacher serves as an example, as a source of inspiration to practise and study. From him or her, you can see that it is possible to liberate yourself from restrictions of your identity, and become a source of love and inspiration. The teacher can also give you practical instructions if your practice is not working well, and advise you on the basis of his or her own experience about what you can perhaps do differently to progress your meditation again.

The second function of the teacher is to hold a mirror in front of you, enabling you to see your hidden obstacles. These are mostly self-protective patterns with which you are still merged, and which are therefore not yet visible in your meditation. The teacher confronts you with these patterns, teaches you to look at them without judgement, and let them dissolve in non-judgemental awareness. Those confrontations can sometimes be painful. A good teacher doesn't pull any punches, because after all he or she doesn't require your admiration or praise in any way, and therefore doesn't need to hold back when confronting you. I explained in earlier chapters that when someone pushes our buttons we're immediately inclined to hold the button-pusher responsible for our painful feelings. But if it's your teacher who pushes your buttons, you know immediately that you'd better look within yourself for the solution to your pain. As a result, the whole process of recognising, letting go, and embracing your ego patterns proceeds much faster than without a teacher.

After some time, a kind of 'love relationship' develops between student and teacher, unlike any other form of relationship. With increasing clarity, you recognise the teacher's natural state and can see that everything he or she says and does is free from self-interest or a hidden agenda, and springs directly from the unconditional source of love of the mind's nature. And the more this helps you to increasingly recognise your own perfect nature, there arises a deep feeling of love and gratitude for the person who has awakened this knowledge and realisation within you.

Another form of Western resistance to spiritual traditions from the East sometimes originates from a psychological perspective. Western psychology's view of the human mind is different from the spiritual view. Psychological methods are aimed at developing or restoring a healthy ego, so that your system of covering self-rejection with other people's love and approval functions optimally. Spiritual methods are aimed at seeing through this covering system, letting go of it, and recognising the perfect state of being that it was concealing. In short, psychology sees the sick mind and wants to heal it; spirituality sees the perfect mind and wants to realise it. Yet there's no reason why you shouldn't use the many psychological developments offered by the West to help you along the spiritual path. On the contrary, those psychological methods are often more attuned to the Western way of thinking and feeling. Even though in themselves they aren't spiritual in character, they can certainly be put to use for a spiritual objective. Because just as an over-busy mind is unable to recognise its own nature, and first needs to become a little calmer, an over-neurotic, fearful and self-rejecting mind can never recognise its own perfect nature. Your ego must already be healthy to some extent, in order for you to transcend it. Your identity must already be somewhat free from serious fears and restrictions before you can discover that it's just an acquired, illusory identity anyway. Thus, psychological methods that are aimed at achieving a healthy identity, combined with spiritual methods which show that every identity is a veil that covers your true state of being, can together form a very effective spiritual practice. It may even be that psychological therapy or training that you've done earlier suddenly 'falls into place' within your spiritual training. Or that spiritual practice over many years suddenly blossoms in your mind as a result of confrontations in an intensive Western workshop.

Perhaps this book will inspire you to follow a spiritual path. It will be the most important decision that you make in your life. But precisely for that reason, it's best to start cautiously. In the chapter on meditation, I mentioned that at first you shouldn't meditate for too long at a time. The same applies if you search for a spiritual teacher or method that suits you: don't try to go too fast. Take a good look around first. Read spiritual books and see which direction appeals to you. Western teachers are often more accessible, easier to understand, but also inclined to be less challenging and confronting, and there's more 'chaff among the wheat': ambitious egos hitching a ride on the growing popularity of (quasi-) spirituality. An Eastern teacher comes from an ancient spiritual tradition, is therefore usually more reliable, but often also more difficult to understand, and the message is sometimes very intermixed with Eastern culture and religion, and therefore initially seems more alien and inaccessible for Westerners. First of all, go to a public lecture or try a workshop or short retreat with a teacher. A good teacher can be recognised from the fact that he or she is inspiring, but sometimes also confrontational, and puts into practice – in both word and deed – what he or she advises others to do. Sometimes it can take years of looking around before you find your teacher, and during that time you can undoubtedly make progress. If you keep looking, you will eventually find a true spiritual teacher, one that you 'click' with and will increasingly grow to love. Then, when you've found that 'outer teacher' it won't be long until you also meet your 'inner teacher', your perfect natural state of being.

So have a good look around, once you've found a teacher or method that works for you, stop your 'spiritual shopping' and devote yourself fully to that one method. Because sooner or later your mind is going to resist whatever method you've chosen, and if you give in to it every time and start looking for something else, you'll keep drifting to and fro between different approaches. It's only when you recognise this resistance as a threshold to deeper layers of your mind, and still remain true to the method, that you can also get through the subtler layers of your identity and achieve true realisation.

If you've already been looking for a while and have tried a variety of spiritual options, and you're questioning whether you're now on the 'right' spiritual path, there's a simple criterion: regular practise. If you practise more or less every day, even if just for five minutes, you're on the path. If you do an intensive spiritual workshop or retreat once a year, but don't practise every day, then you're not yet really on the spiritual path. You're perhaps gathering inspiration, and that is very valuable. But if you seriously want to recognise your perfect nature, then you have to start practising every day, for a short or long time depending on your experience and circumstances. We've had our veiling patterns for a very long time and their functioning is automatic. You can only see through them and learn to let go of them if you regularly go within yourself, let your mind come to rest and get to know its clear and loving nature. Although at first it may seem to be a kind of spiritual chore, very soon your practice will become the most beautiful time of each day, the 'moment for yourself' in the most profound sense. Those moments will expand and join together until you never lose yourself, whatever happens, and your everyday life is enacted in the joyful recognition of the essence of every experience: loving and non-judgemental awareness.